# PATTON'S BEST

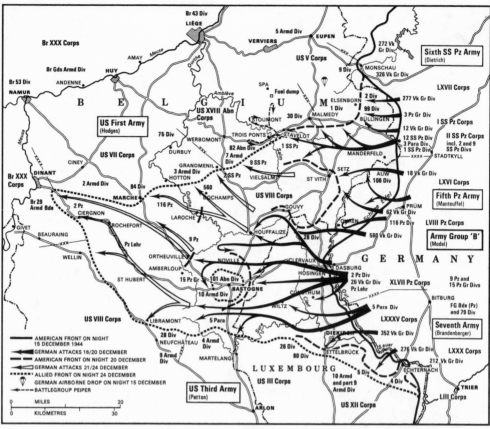

**Map legend (top map):**

- AMERICAN FRONT ON NIGHT 15 DECEMBER 1944
- GERMAN ATTACKS 16/20 DECEMBER
- AMERICAN FRONT ON NIGHT 20 DECEMBER
- GERMAN ATTACKS 21/24 DECEMBER
- ALLIED FRONT ON NIGHT 24 DECEMBER
- GERMAN AIRBORNE DROP ON NIGHT 15 DECEMBER
- BATTLEGROUP PEIPER

MILES 0 — 20
KILOMETRES 0 — 30

**Top map labels:**

Br 43 Div — LIÈGE — 5 Armd Div — EUPEN — Br XXX Corps — VERVIERS — US V Corps — 272 Vk Gr Div — Sixth SS Pz Army (Dietrich) — AMAY — Meuse — Outhe — 9 Div — MONSCHAU — 326 Vk Gr Div — LXVII Corps — Br Gds Armd Div — HUY — ANDENNE — SPA — Fuel dump — Amblève — ELSENBORN — 2 Div — 277 Vk Gr Div — Br 53 Div — NAMUR — US XVIII Abn Corps — US First Army (Hodges) — STOUMONT — 30 Div — 1 Div — 99 Div — MALMEDY — BÜLLINGEN — 3 Pz Gr Div — I SS Pz Corps — 12 Vk Gr Div — 75 Div — WERBOMONT — TROIS PONTS — STAVELOT — 1 SS Pz — 12 SS Pz Div — II SS Pz Corps incl. 2 and 9 SS Pz Divs — 3 Para Div — 1 SS Pz Div — STADTKYLL — CINEY — DURBUY — 82 Abn Div — 7 Armd Div — 9 SS Pz — MANDERFELD — US VII Corps — GRANDMENIL — 3 Armd Div — HOTTON — 2 SS Pz — VIELSALM — SETZ — AUW — 18 Vk Gr Div — LXVI Corps — Br XXX Corps — DINANT — 2 Armd Div — 84 Div — MARCHE — 560 — BOCHAMPS — ST VITH — 106 Div — Fifth Pz Army (Manteuffel) — Br 29 Armd Bde — 2 Pz — CIERGNON — 116 Pz — LAROCHE — GOUVY — 62 Vk Gr Div — PRÜM — Army Group 'B' (Model) — ROCHEFORT — HOUFFALIZE — 116 Pz Div — LVIII Pz Corps — BEAURAING — Pz Lehr — 9 Pz — 28 Div — 560 Vk Gr Div — WELLIN — ORTHEUVILLE — NOVILLE — CLERVAUX — DASBURG — GERMANY — AMBERLOUP — 15 Pz Gr — 101 Abn Div — HÖSINGEN — 2 Pz Div — 26 Vk Gr Div — Pz Lehr — XLVII Pz Corps — 9 Pz and 15 Gr Divs — ST HUBERT — BASTOGNE — 10 Armd Div — CONSTHUM — BITBURG — FG Bde (Pz) and 79 Div — WILTZ — 5 Para Div — US VIII Corps — LIBRAMONT — 5 Para — LXXXV Corps — Seventh Army (Brandenberger) — 28 Div — NEUFCHÂTEAU — 4 Armd Div — DIEKIRCH — 352 Vk Gr Div — 9 Armd Div — MARTELANGE — 26 Div — 80 Div — ETTELBRÜCK — Sauer — 276 Vk Gr Div — LXXX Corps — LUXEMBOURG — 10 Armd and part 9 Armd Div — 5 Div — 4 Div — ECHTERNACH — 212 Vk Gr Div — TRIER — US Third Army (Patton) — US III Corps — US XII Corps — LIII Corps — ARLON

## The Battle of the Ardennes.

Maps reprinted by permission of
G. P. Putnam's Sons, New York,
from *Atlas of the Second World
War* by Brigadier Peter Young.
Cartography by Richard Natkiel.

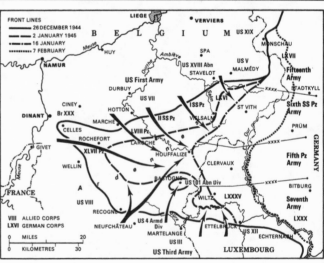

**Bottom map legend:**

FRONT LINES
- 26 DECEMBER 1944
- 2 JANUARY 1945
- 16 JANUARY
- 7 FEBRUARY

VIII — ALLIED CORPS
LXVI — GERMAN CORPS

MILES 0 — 20
KILOMETRES 0 — 30

**Bottom map labels:**

LIÈGE — VERVIERS — US XIX — BELGIUM — HUY — Meuse — Outhe — Amblève — SPA — MONSCHAU — NAMUR — US XVIII Abn — STAVELOT — US V — MALMÉDY — LXVII — Fifteenth Army — STADTKYLL — US First Army — DURBUY — US VII — 1 SS Pz — LXVI — ST VITH — Sixth SS Pz Army — CINEY — Br XXX — HOTTON — II SS Pz — VIELSALM — PRÜM — DINANT — MARCHE — LVIII Pz — CELLES — ROCHEFORT — LAROCHE — GERMANY — GIVET — XLVII Pz — HOUFFALIZE — Fifth Pz Army — WELLIN — CLERVAUX — BITBURG — FRANCE — US VIII — A — d — BASTOGNE — US 101 Abn Div — WILTZ — LXXXV — Seventh Army — RECOGNE — US 4 Armd Div — ETTELBRÜCK — LXXX — NEUFCHÂTEAU — MARTELANGE — US XII — ECHTERNACH — US III — US Third Army — LUXEMBOURG

# PATTON'S BEST:
## AN INFORMAL
## HISTORY OF THE
## 4TH ARMORED DIVISION

by Nat Frankel and Larry Smith

HAWTHORN BOOKS, INC.
Publishers/NEW YORK
A Howard & Wyndham Company

For Fred Frankel,
whose patience made this book possible

# Contents

# 6

# Chronology

| | |
|---|---|
| January 5, 1942 | 4th Armored reorganized as autonomous unit at Pine Camp, New York |
| December 1942–June 1943 | |
| | 4th Armored trains at Camp Ibis in the Mojave |
| June 14, 1943 | Transfer to Camp Bowie, Texas |
| December 1943 | Transfer to Myles Standish Camp, Massachusetts |
| December 29, 1943 | Most of 4th Armored sails from Boston |
| January–July 1944 | 4th Armored in England |
| July 1944 | 4th Armored lands at Utah Beach |
| July–August 31, 1944 | 4th Armored strikes across Normandy, Brittany, and northern France; reaches banks of the Meuse |
| July 28, 1944 | Captures first town, Coutances |
| July 31, 1944 | Takes key city of Avranches |
| August 2, 1944 | Heavy fighting at Rennes |
| August 7, 1944 | Moves against Lorient |
| August 25, 1944 | Takes Troyes and a bridgehead across the Seine |
| Early September 1944 | |
| | 4th Armored crosses Meuse |
| Mid-September 1944 | 4th Armored crosses Moselle |
| November 25, 1944 | Patton takes Metz |

| | |
|---|---|
| December 3, 1944 | John Wood relieved of command |
| December 8, 1944 | Battle of Singling ends as Third and Seventh Armies link up |
| December 20, 1944 | 4th Armored at Arlon, where the heaviest segment of the run to Bastogne will begin |
| December 24, 1944 | Heavy fighting at Chaumont |
| December 26, 1944 | 4th Armored reaches Bastogne and rescues 101st Airborne |
| Late February 1945 | 4th Armored smashes West Wall, or Siegfried Line |
| March 4, 1945 | Starts from Bitburg for Koblenz and gets there less than three days later |
| March 1945 | Palatinate campaign |
| March 25, 1945 | 4th Armored crosses Rhine |
| Late March–April 1945 | Task Force Baum attacks PW camp well behind enemy lines. A handful survive. |
| Early April 1945 | 4th Armored attains first American liberation of a concentration camp at Ohrdruf |
| May 1945 | 4th Armored outside Prague as war ends |
| May–June 1945 | Detach service with CIA (OSS) |

# Breakdown of the 4th Armored Division

8th Tank Battalion
35th Tank Battalion
37th Tank Battalion
10th Armored Infantry Battalion
51st Armored Infantry Battalion
53rd Armored Infantry Battalion
24th Armored Engineer Battalion
22nd Armored Field Artillery Battalion
66th Armored Field Artillery Battalion
94th Armored Field Artillery Battalion
25th Cavalry Reconnaissance Squadron, Mechanized
126th Armored Ordnance Maintenance Battalion
46th Armored Medical Battalion
Headquarters and Headquarters Battery
Division Artillery
CCA Headquarters and Headquarters Company
Reserve Command
Division Headquarters Company
144th Armored Signal Company
Trains Headquarters and Headquarters Company
Forward Echelon, 4th Armored Division Headquarters
Rear Echelon, 4th Armored Division Headquarters
4th Armored Division Military Police Platoon
4th Armored Division Band

# PATTON'S BEST

# 1

# Roosevelt's Butchers

Pick up any German soldier from Normandy to Brittany, from the Rhine to Prague, and ask him about the 4th Armored Division. He may not know at first what you're talking about, but mention Roosevelt's butchers and he'll respond immediately. He'll know then. If he has seen us, if he's fought against us, he'll shake his head in despair and quote you chapter and verse: how we move, what we look like, how we can cut through terrain and blockade like butter. If he has never seen us, if his only knowledge of us has been word of mouth (which must have spread through the German ranks like typhus), then his eyes will widen and he'll speak of us as if he were a nineteenth-century child in a Boston schoolhouse imagining the Apaches.

Roosevelt's butchers . . . If I call the 4th Armored "Patton's best," my German counterparts chose to express it differently. Who knows to what ends of the earth the Germans had spread the gospel of our terror? I can well imagine German soldiers gathering for drinks in some far-flung corner of the war. Someone mentions my division and, before the glasses are refilled, the conversation extends to fable. Yet the war is over, and in the thirty-odd years since—thirty very odd years—the 4th

Armored has begun to recede from memory, backward, into fragments traceable only in gargantuan history texts, into yearbooks and commemorations read only by the men who were there and who cannot help but cherish their recollections of apocalypse. And so I'm writing a book, an effort to make a legend live again, a hopeful attempt to make some readers marvel at what was genuinely marvelous.

Roosevelt's butchers . . . I remember the German soldier we captured in Brittany. It was that early in the war. Not four months after landing in France, and our legend had been formulated! The prisoner was a lanky, nervous private who had seen our tanks creeping up over a hill and who had not even bothered to run. He had thrown down his gun and shot his long arms straight up. His whole torso was extended, and his legs were rigid. He looked like an ironing board.

My friend George Cardge was chatting with him later. George was always interested in people, and the notion of an enemy soldier fascinated him. Whenever he found one who knew some English, he couldn't resist. "Your company's pretty good," George said. "In fact, your whole goddamn army is pretty good." George smiled broadly, without the least trace of condescension.

The prisoner remained silent for a moment or two. He was apparently nervous. Finally he spoke—rather indiscreetly, I might add, considering what he thought of us. "And you are the butchers?"

"What?" George bellowed. "What are you talking about?"

"Roosevelt's butchers . . ."

"Hey, wait a minute!"

And then we learned, if not that day then the next, that this soldier was not the only one in the German army who used this phraseology. Some weeks later another prisoner told us something equally interesting. We were teasing him, asking him what it felt like to be in the hands of "Roosevelt's butchers." He said he wasn't afraid to die. He also mumbled something about what nice guys we seemed to be and that we probably wouldn't kill him without cause. We laughed and gave him a cigarette. In a few minutes he was more comfortable.

"What did you do?" he asked one of us.

"What do you mean, what did I do?"

"Why did they put you in prison?"

"Prison? What prison?"

"You were not in prison?"

"Not even close."

"Then, why did they put you with Roosevelt's butchers?"

And so it was. The Germans thought we were all ex-cons emptied out of San Quentin and Sing Sing to practice on the Germans the same savagery we had committed against our own countrymen. We were cannon fodder in their eyes, desperate men with nothing to lose and no reason to fear death. Fine, we didn't correct the prisoner. Let them think it. Nothing is as terrifying as a man who doesn't mind dying. As long as they thought that of the 4th Armored, we would have a considerable psychological advantage, the same advantage the North Koreans had in the Korean War. But, of course, they *really* weren't afraid to die, and we were, all of us. The 4th Armored was totally human.

Later we would learn more about our own reputation. The myth that we were all ex-cons derived from our personal appearance as much as from our combat skills. The Germans had never seen a Mohican haircut before. One day a redneck private had turned up wearing one, much to the amusement of city slickers like myself. But George Cardge, who was from Wheeling, West Virginia, assumed a put-upon, defensive air and berated me for showing too little respect for my southern comrade. Within the next day or two the whole division was crawling with them: Mohican hairdos in all the colors of the Confederate flag!

Now, the Germans were great ones for shaving the heads of the condemned. When they saw our Mohicans peeking out of our turrets, they naturally assumed that the wardens of New

York and Illinois and California had followed the same standard operating procedure used by Nazi commandants. And so the legend of Roosevelt's butchers deepened and was given a terrifyingly visible testimony.

And no doubt there were times that we acted like butchers. The longer you're in a war, the more your moral attentiveness wears down. You become less scrupulous, or at least less assiduous. Well, all soldiers are expected to behave like butchers. Eventually you become one. I am thinking of a particular incident as we approached the Battle of Singling in late 1944. I was in my turret at the time, guiding four prisoners whose lazy march accompanied the movement of my tank. A jeep drove up and an infantry sergeant (tank divisions always traveled and fought in concert with infantry detachments) yelled up at me.

"Those prisoners holding you up?"

"Damn right," I yelled back.

"You want me to take them off your hands?"

"Sure."

He crowded all four of them into his jeep and drove it over an embankment to our left. I drove on in my tank until I couldn't see the jeep or the prisoners. But my progress was suddenly halted by the startling sound of unexpected gunfire. I swirled around in the turret and saw the noncom driving back toward me, alone. He smiled as he drove past, smiled and waved.

But if we were Roosevelt's butchers, we were also Patton's best. I don't want to sound like a senile old soldier exaggerating the glories of past campaigns, but I would suggest, with all due respect to every other fighting unit since Bunker Hill, that the 4th Armored Division was the greatest single combat force in American history. I have often thought back over all my country's military involvements, and I am hard pressed to remember any body of fighting men who were comparable. World War I certainly did not see any, nor did Korea, Vietnam, nor the nineteenth-century wars. If anyone could have stood in our shoes, it would have to be some other World

War II detachment, perhaps Merrill's Marauders. But we were surely the best in Europe, and I am absolutely certain that, as far as celerity and persistence are concerned, we were the apples of Uncle Sam's eye. On any given day any one man can fight as well as any other man, but we hammered away for a year at the finest panzer divisions, sped across formidable terrain in every sort of weather, and never stopped shooting.

No, I've got to believe that we were the best. George S. Patton would have agreed, and Omar Bradley and Anthony MacAuliffe and Maxwell Taylor wouldn't have argued. In fact, Patton said it: "There has never been such a superb fighting organization as the Fourth Armored Division." So if I have a tendency toward hyperbole, how much more so the commander of the Third Army, an expert historian who cannot even find our superiors in the annals of the finest Roman legions or British warships!

It is not my purpose in this book to write a formal history of the division. Perhaps some professional historian will feel impelled to do so. I hope that will be the case and that this memoir will be of use to him. It is my purpose to render the texture of war in general—and, specifically, to give you some feeling of what it was like to follow the 4th Armored from Normandy to Prague. In so doing, I hope this magnificent legend can be reborn.

I will, moreover, presume to punctuate history, to follow the division in its frequently horrific journey through time and space, and emphasize aspects of the war often ignored by historians. I cannot, of course, omit the Battle of the Bulge and our participation in the famous rescue of the First Army at Bastogne, nor can I pretend that the actual crossing of the Rhine was anything less than momentous. But there are footnotes to history that deserve something more than the desultory treatment they're usually afforded. The Battle of Singling, the crossing of the Meuse, the fight for Metz, the first American liberation of a concentration camp at Ohrdruf— these events are no less significant in the life of the division.

One of the benefits of such an approach is that war is thus

seen from the dog soldier's perspective. From the standpoint of a historian, Bastogne deserves a thousand pages and Singling considerably fewer. But to any man who fought the war, whose blood fills the historian's inkwell, Singling is as significant. Something that feels monumentally important while you're there may not, in the long strategic run of things, be that important. But I'm writing this book from the goddamn basement, where the scale that measures men and events is far less Olympian and far more concrete, a concretion composed of death and suffering and obscure glory. If it *feels* monumental, it *is* monumental.

And so the history is "informal," so much so that I have changed some names to protect the guilty. When, for example, you meet Ernie Jacobson, who had been a gunman for the mob back in the States, you can rely on the fact that "Ernie Jacobson" ain't the name his mama gave him! Yet he belongs here, because, like so many of the men whose real names I'm proud to use, men like George Cardge and John Wood and Bob Saville, he *was* the war. But, of course, so were Roosevelt and Eisenhower. To understand as mighty a fact as war, one must see things from both perspectives. Read all that they have to say about Ike and Patton and learn things about Bastogne I couldn't tell you. But know the George Cardges as well, for, without them, war is but a series of lines on a map.

And there are moments, rare and profound moments, when the two perspectives intersect, when history is palpable in the basement, or when the gods suddenly start talking and acting like men. General John Wood incarnated the latter moment; he was with us in the basement but lived on Olympus, and he spent the war balancing the two worlds in his large and heroic heart. Or there are moments when the dog soldier suddenly sees everything in cool and frightening totality, when suddenly you fire your gun at Bastogne and you can hear Hitler contemplate his irrevocable destiny as he orders his men to prepare the bunker.

The 4th Armored Division was organized as an autonomous unit in early 1942 at Pine Camp in upstate New York: an oddly idyllic setting to serve as a spawning ground for an American president's personal "butchers." Of course, there's often an incongruity between war and the pastoral environment that either bears it or witnesses it; by 1945 we would be totally familiar with this awful paradox. The fact is, magnolias running with blood are more frightening in their way than frozen toes in unyielding snow.

I had spent the latter part of 1941 at Pine Camp as well. I was discharged on December 4, and I went home to Queens— but not right home. I was a happy man. I had done my duty, and I could now freely use my time until civilian responsibilities would lay their claim. I started drinking at Pine Camp and didn't stop until White Plains. In fact, it took me three days to get back downstate. I got home on a Sunday morning, hungover but ecstatic. I took off my heavy, heavy boots, wiggled my toes, and turned on the radio. Boom! Tojo!

So back to Pine Camp. We did our preliminary training there, interrupted only by an AWOL trip I took to Canada with my good friend Bob Saville. There we crashed an officers' club and managed to get ourselves treated like American VIPs. So far it was fun. Then the entire 4th Armored was shipped to Fort Knox for motorcycle maneuvers, followed by more training in the rural areas of Tennessee.

Camp Ibis in the Mojave was next. It was bases such as Ibis that first inspired Benny Siegel to build Las Vegas, but I never saw it. From the latter part of 1942 to June of 1943, we trained and watched the dust storms blow. In fact, Camp Ibis would have been a marvelous training experience for the North African war. It was my only taste of what that kind of fighting must have been like, and just that taste of swirling sand and palpatating heat has given me a lifelong admiration for T. E. Lawrence and Bernard Montgomery and all the rats who ever fought in deserts.

Next was Camp Bowie in Texas, where the 4th Armored was further organized and now included the 8th Tank Battalion. There were German prisoners at Camp Bowie, many of whom spoke English. One of them seemed particularly interesting. He looked cocky and would treat his captors as if they were at *his* mercy. A kind of condescending pity constantly hung about him. One day I couldn't stand it anymore, and I engaged him in conversation—small talk at first, an unsure effort on my part to plumb these odd depths.

He told me that the had been captured by the British and transferred to American care via some small island in the Atlantic. I asked him about his hometown, which was Munich, and he sang that city's glories for a boring half hour or so. Then he finally decided he might want to know what town in American I was from. New York, I told him.

"I'm sorry," he said.

"What are you sorry about?" I asked.

It turned out that Dr. Goebbels had informed a certain section of the military population (and probably the civilian population as well) that a new German weapon, incredible in its proportions, had completely obliterated New York City—and that only a few more months of manufacture would be necessary before other American cities, including Washington, would be similarly wasted. Why, the American political and military commands had already beat a hasty retreat to North Dakota or Walla Walla or Utica. (Hot Springs I could have believed!) I told him he was crazy, that first of all, I had just talked to my sister in New York by phone, and second, no such weapon would ever exist. He patted me on my hopeless head and continued to sympathize. My sister was dead. That was someone else's voice on the phone, trying to keep my spirits up!

But what interests me most in retrospect is not the lunacy of the Nazi propaganda machine but the ingredient of truth infused into this madness. How naive we both were! Him, to believe that New York had been destroyed, and myself, to believe that no such weapon was possible. Now I know how the greatest of liars—and Goebbels was precisely that—always begin with a possible truth.

I am also struck by what a cliché this incident may seem to any reader who has seen a similar exchange portrayed in a movie or fictionalized in a cheap novel. And yet, like the big lies, clichés begin with truth. This is nowhere more evident than in efforts to comprehend the consistency of warfare. That a German soldier could be so totally propagandized—that cliché was once a living fact. I can even think of a more germane example. After we crossed the Rhine, our lines were constantly infiltrated by German soldiers wearing American uniforms and jabberring English like William F. Buckley. How did we trap them? Think back over all the Errol Flynn and John Wayne movies you've seen and try to guess. Right! You've got it! We would ask them if DiMaggio was still pitching with the Cubs! Even my sister, the one who got blown up by the A-bomb in New York, knew that Joe was no pitcher and certainly not with the Cubs! Something about this snare appealed to Hollywood; they made a cliché out of what once had been a very sanguine and very human facet of the military experience.

I wonder if that German is still sympathizing with me; I wonder if he ever went to New York, and if so, did he insist that its skyline was nothing more than a ruse by the Pentagon to keep up our people's spirits? We left him behind in Texas, nodding his head and sympathizing, and the 4th Armored went to Myles Standish Camp in Thornton, Massachusetts. Then Boston, then an ocean, then England.

And, in July of 1944, we landed in France, at a place called Utah Beach. Others had done the same one month earlier, a day on which an entire continent had been invaded. The wake of that invasion, our visit to the silent aftermath of D day, was one of the most haunting experiences in the life of the 4th

Armored Division. A piercing silence enveloped us. A thin smoky vapor rose up from the beach and invested the air; it was like some ancient pyre on which terrible sacrifices had been made to mammoth gods—and on which those gods themselves had perished.

The carcasses of the gods were everywhere. Here an upturned jeep. There a sunken ship, its prow jutting against the first shore of Europe. We unloaded our gear in silence, though occasionally you could hear someone mutter, "Well, here we are," or "It must have been something." It was hard to imagine that any war could possibly lay ahead of us. How could it not have ended here? How could there be any sort of follow-up to such an eerie scene? What it must have been like for the men who cleared away the corpses, here and at Omaha! And this, this was only the first blood, no more than a slap in the face before the brawl broke out—for the war was yet to be won, at Saint-Lô and at Bastogne, in Rome, in Berlin.

Our predecessors, those amphibious heroes who had cleared this path for us, had marched on, widening an even broader terrain. So we marched on, unopposed for miles. We stopped at a place called Carentan, and in the distance we heard the first ominous rumble. I walked in front of my tank and saw the billowy fire rise above the leas ahead. There it was, visible from Carentan. There it was, the thing called World War II.

We waited at Carentan. It was there that a vital event occurred, vital in ways we would not be able to assess for weeks. A new army was formed there, to which the 8th Tank Battalion and the 4th Armored Division would be assigned for the rest of the war. It was the Third Army, its commander a prima donna famous to me at that time only as the man who had so gratuitously slapped a hysterical soldier. Within months, however, the 4th Armored, and all the other divisions and companies similarly assigned, would have an additional name. Whenever other units from other armies would pass us on the road and shout "Who are you?" we'd call back, "Georgie's boys!"

It was at that time too that my friendship with four dog soldiers was cemented. I have already mentioned Bob Saville and George Cardge; Bob I was still close to from the Pine Camp days. And George became like a kid brother; before we ever saw combat, I was already feeling protective toward him. And then there were two others. Andy Cammerrary was a baker from Brooklyn, a solid human being, a dependable friend and brave soldier. Finally, there was Paul Glaz, a man I could imagine doing very well in civilian life. He didn't look like an officer; he looked more like a man who could rise to the top of any business.

From the very first moment we left Thornton for England, we assumed, as did most of the men, that we would die in Europe. Death is not something a soldier toys with, but only the foolish ones expect ever to return. There is great anguish in looking around at your friends, assessing the kind of husbands and workers they are capable of being, the sort of personal loyalty and laughter they generate, and knowing that they will be dead tomorrow or the next day. It was not something I could afford to dwell on when I looked at Andy or Bob or Paul or George, but it remained in the back of my mind. But we were lucky. Only one of us died.

When the war was over, I would spend the better years of my life driving a cab in New York City. An odd profession for a tank commander, but there is great poetic justice in it! In peace as in war, I would drive, not walk or run or sit, through the alleyways of hell. My tank would follow the 4th Armored through Brittany, across the Meuse and the Moselle, up to Metz and back to a town called Arracourt, over into the Belfort Gap, and up to Bastogne, across the Siegfried Line and the borders of Germany, across the Rhine to Ohrdruf, stopping finally outside Prague.

And what did I win? I won an opportunity to drive my cab,

up Eighth Avenue, weaving between the pimps and whores; up to Harlem and the leaden-eyed children of the night, back down to the Lower East Side and over to Wall Street, where some men invest in war; cross the bridge maybe to Brooklyn and thank God Czar Lepke is dead; back to Manhattan and the gaudy Chinatown streets or the mob-run blocks of Little Italy. My mess tent would be the Belmore Cafeteria, where other soldiers would gather for coffee before combat. There's a moral here to my life: Never let your feet touch ground!

Yet the images of the first hell outlast anything the streets of New York can show. A tank blows up and a man jumps out of the turret. He runs along the ground toward the nearest friendly tank, his head down, his arms dangling. A dead infantryman lies in his way. A German tank advances from his rear. He picks up the dead man's gun and fires at the advancing enemy, even as he runs backward toward his own. That man, whose name I can't recall, personifies the 4th Armored Division.

A man lies dead in the turret. Suddenly his body is propelled upward by an unseen hand. The corpse dashes to the ground. The man who had flung him out replaces him. Then he, too, slumps over. Then the tank stops.

An infantryman's legs catch on fire, but it takes him a minute or two to realize it. He is a walking flame. But then the fire reaches his waist and he screams and dies.

In his first taste of combat a young soldier's hands have to be pried loose from a pole to which he has grabbed on. He is too scared to even whimper. We loosen his fingers one by one. As we loosen each finger, someone else has to hold it to make sure he won't use it to grab back on. But within a week that soldier is fighting bravely, killing with as much nobility as one can kill. That man also personifies the 4th Armored Division.

And what would it all come to by the time Patton's best, or Roosevelt's butchers, would disband? It would come to 90,354 Germans captured. It would come to 13,640 Germans killed. We'd wound about 30,000 more, take 579 tanks, 3,668 other vehicles, 603 artillery and antitank guns, and 103 locomotives. We'd shoot down 128 Nazi planes. Take about thirty major cities and too many towns and villages to count. Get enough medals to deflate the price of silver. Earn the respect of every major military figure in the world. In about a year.

# 2

# Voulez-Vous Coucher avec Moi?

It was Omar Bradley's idea, and it was called Operation Cobra, a master plan for the whole Brittany campaign. It would begin on the Cotentin Peninsula, where we were grouping. We would head for the town of Avranches and then fan out through that town in four different directions, cutting the heart of France. Avranches would thus serve as a bottleneck, and the different forces issuing from it would be like a serpent's fangs. The 4th Armored would be the middle fang; it would hiss on down to the port cities of Vannes and Lorient.

An air strike would lead the way, cause as much disruption as possible before the infantry and armored divisions would begin the task of reappropriating French soil. In late July of 1944 we were perched along the Seves River in Normandy, watching our planes do their hectic work no more than four or five miles ahead of us. It was the goddamn Fourth of July, only twenty days late.

It was also my first taste of that very odd phenomenon, finding the face of war aesthetically pleasing. The sky was illuminated with profound bursts of orange juxtaposed to darting billows of yellow. For an instant there was rigid contrast between the colors, like two garish pillows pasted together. Then a gradual merging of the two, and soon a third color emerged, a deeper yellow than anything I'd ever seen. Death and destruction seemed to be very insignificant factors in it all. The horror was not abstracted away; it was merely overwhelmed by the dazzling display. And we were firing into it all, the black death of our guns hardly denting the colorful phantasmagoria. Five, ten miles away, beneath the exquisite clouds, German soldiers—husbands and fathers, philosophers and degenerates, short-order cooks and businessmen—were dying in this, this odd dream of a Michelangelo or a Gauguin.

We moved on. I was still jittery with my first taste of combat. Normandy had been light, but I can only say that in retrospect. After we left Carentan, I thought there was a sniper in every tree, a mine under every clod of earth. By the time we left the Seves, I was somewhat more relaxed—now there were only snipers in every third tree and a mine under every fifth pebble. Eventually I wouldn't even be thinking about mines or snipers; I'd merely be cleaning them out as efficiently as I could, as if I were brushing my teeth. Of course, if luck is with you, your gums don't bleed.

But the road out of Normandy was indeed mined, considerably more than the Carentan area had been. I don't remember anyone getting killed on the road, but we lost two trucks and a tank had to be retreaded. The worst part of these explosions was that they made us acutely aware of their potential and their probable numerousness. This was the excruciating aspect of those first few days. You stare at the ground and wonder where not to walk. What part of this dust, or this rich loam, carries death within it? The earth itself becomes your enemy. But the seasoned warrior tires of fearing the earth, so he takes what comes.

We passed through a town called Periers, which our planes had cleared before us. It was the first time I had ever seen a totally destroyed village. Everything was skeletal. Houses with just the girders erect, piles of rubble accumulating along the sidewalks and spilling out into the street, a seared plain where once there had been a park. A friend of mine who had fought in Italy, and who had seen many such villages in the war, told me of a visit he made to Managua, Nicaragua, a short time after their enormous earthquake. He said he had never seen anything like it. Well, I suppose there are some horrors even mankind cannot surpass.

After Periers we had our first real fight for control of a town, the town of Coutances. At this stage in our career all we could do was fire where everyone else seemed to be firing. We were not sufficiently experienced to develop in our own mind's eye an encapsulated picture of the whole battle. Perhaps a combatant is never able to comprehend the whole face of a battle, but he does begin to pick up certain hints that give him some idea of what is happening. Maybe the enemy's fire from the right isn't as strong as it should be, maybe there's a premature surcease, and you figure, with probable accuracy, that the tide has turned. Or perhaps a few German tanks are advancing with unusual boldness, so you estimate that this is the enemy's most important moment. And if you're right, you, the tank commander, you win the fight for your side—for your adrenalin works up and you react to the enemy's vital thrust with ever greater force. There are so many elements and men and strata of command involved in even the smallest victory, or defeat.

As early as Coutances we were able to feel the first release that comes with apparent victory. And when we did, we pushed harder, like an amateur fighter who scores a knockout punch but feels impelled to score a few more times before his opponent finally hits the canvas. And that is amateurism. Notice how the really great heavyweight simply walks away after the one punch he knows to be the crucial one. At Coutances, on the other hand, we just kept shooting and driving, shooting and driving, and when word got around that the enemy was evacuating, we shot harder and drove faster. Two months later we would have slowed down a bit and smoked a cigarette.

Coutances became the first of a long string of hard-won villages bled for by American flesh but obscure now to American memory. There was only one more German position between us and Avranches, a little place called La Haye Pesnel. We took it the same way we had taken Coutances. There was little to change. Just hold your ground and shoot. Then move. After we took the town, I saw an American soldier bleeding his life away on a stretcher, moaning pitifully until the medics finally took him away. I had never seen that before, not in such a prolonged and wretched scenario. And when the medics lifted him up, he starting moaning more loudly, and then he was screaming, so that I was still aware of him fifty yards away. I wonder if it's better to die in a big battle, a Bastogne or an Iwo Jima, than in a small fight for a small town. The automatic response, of course, is that it doesn't mean a goddamn thing to the man who dies, but a nagging thought persists in my mind. I can't help but think it's more dignified to be buried at Waterloo than in Kookamonga somewhere.

Avranches was a big battle, and, as I've indicated, it would serve an important purpose; it would be a starting point for a comprehensive and mighty campaign. The Germans had four divisions and a regiment defending it, and they were pulling every trick in the book. No doubt there was a stable line, but it didn't appear that way to us. We seemed to be surrounded by invisible Germans, with fire pouring down on us from every angle. A bird's-eye view may have disclosed (in fact, it probably would have disclosed) a relentless American push against a faltering German defense. But I felt about as relentless as a stick of butter in the Gobi Desert, and the Germans seemed as faltering as Willie Mays rounding third.

What made it worse was that the Luftwaffe was having a pretty good day. In fact, Avranches may have been Goering's last stand. Never again would we encounter such tumult from the sky; John Wood would see to that. But Avranches was very different. I saw firsthand how effective aerial cover is, an effectiveness that no soldier can ever really gauge until he is on the receiving end. A kind of arc of death encircles you. You've got these enormous German tanks and artillery guns blowing your nose, while at any minute a bomb may tumble from an unseen plane in a darkened sky.

The Luftwaffe made a direct hit not twenty yards from me. The tank exploded and the men inside were incinerated. And suddenly the bodies began to pile up around me. I would later learn that the gradual mixing of German and American corpses is sometimes—if you yourself are moving forward—a good sign. It means that Americans are falling on ground where once only Germans had fallen. The obscene coupling of mutilated bodies with the men who had mutilated them often signifies incipient victory. And in case you haven't heard, it's always better to win.

After Avranches I was a real soldier, and the 4th Armored, whose talent had been evident from its inception, could now face any combat. It had won its stripes, and I would learn what it meant to actually adapt to combat. I saw five Germans on foot and an American gunner cut them down. I saw men wiggle out of burning tanks, only to die a moment later. I saw a German plane smoldering on the ground—perhaps it had just crashed, a victim of faulty mechanism—with twenty unrecognizable carcasses strewn around it, unlucky soldiers shattered between the impact of machine and earth. And I saw infantrymen running and ducking and falling and sometimes getting up again. Suddenly I wasn't afraid. Something had tightened in my gut and I continued shooting. Then fear returned again, and then another tightening, another personal push against the enemy, and death was so close I couldn't fear it. The scar tissue had formed around my heart, what would happen would happen.

And then I learned something else as well, that a battle doesn't simply end; it continues sporadically until the next battle. In fact, part of the distinction of my division was its constant embattlement. You fight for a town, you take it, and then there are people inside the town who have to be killed, captured, or driven out. Avranches typified this. Indeed, Avranches was tougher than most of the towns we would later occupy. Elsewhere, we could simply blow away pockets of resistance huddled in a corner or configured in the main square. But Avranches was a labyrinthine little city, and the Germans had hidden tanks in every nook and cranny.

Quiet, for thirty or forty yards. Suddenly there are four panzer refugees encircling you. One may have come from a back alley. Another may have hurtled out of a ramshackle house. You have to hold them off until your friends arrive, and then you've got a fight on your hands. The Germans surround you, and then your friends encircle the Germans.

These enemy tanks were not left behind in order to wreak a kamikazelike havoc and then destroy themselves. No, they really had no choice. The German flight from Avranches was a chaotic and ill-fated one. Their lines had been broken, and the time they needed in order to organize an orderly and efficient evacuation was simply not available. Not only, then, did we continue our fight against hidden tanks within the town, but units of the 4th Armored were ordered to intercept the German withdrawal as well. As a result, the sound of fire from the suburbs was constant. Our tanks were going back and forth up and down the German line, picking them off wherever possible. It may have been here that the 4th Armored first got into the habit of devastating the enemy's rear, a habit we would maintain throughout the war, so much so that many observers have compared John Wood to Jeb Stuart, the master of rear attack.

It was also during the German flight from Avranches that a 4th Armored gunner became the first of us to win the Distinguished Service Cross. He was Red Whitson, a hell-bent-for-leather redneck from Indianapolis. Attached to Company B, he found himself isolated from his comrades and had to face off a unit of Germans. It must have been cinematic. The

way it was later told, and confirmed by many cool heads not
prone to exaggeration, Red was almost alone with his gun,
spraying fire and killing fifty or more Germans. Then he was
shot in the hand and could no longer manipulate his weapon
as effectively. He was finally killed, but not before he had
obliterated enemy soldiers, trucks, jeeps, and horses.

Did I say horses? Indeed, even as late as 1944, the Germans
were still using mounted units. Of course, they did not base
resistance or attack on mounted forces, but apparently they
still found them useful enough for quick transport, for pomp
and ceremony, for whatever. Later on in Brittany, closer to
Lorient, my company would meet a lot of horses—but I'll get to
that later on.

Avranches did more than simply earn us our stripes and
accustom us to Armageddon. After the fight we felt like what
we were; we felt like the 4th Armored Division. Reports of the
entire outcome made our achievement almost shockingly clear
to us. Fourteen Germans had died for every one American. We
had smashed about five divisions, including the somewhat
vaunted 5th Para Division. That unit would be reorganized
much later on, and we would meet its resurrection at
Bastogne.

Our territorial gain was, moreover, something to be proud
of. There were pockets of Germans behind us that others could
now pick off like plums. We had secured the Selune River as
far south as Ducey. Indeed, the whole campaign seemed to be
in a state of consolidation. With such information in hand, we
could not help but draw our own conclusions. We were thinking of ourselves as an elite unit, and, of course, prophecies
have a way of fulfilling themselves.

So the Nazis began their flight southward, and we, with the
rest of the Third Army, began our journey in that very same
direction. It's been called the Saint Lô breakthrough and the
Avranches breakthrough. We called it something different.
Ten miles outside Avranches we already had the feeling of
constant movement, or pursuit. We'd catch German stragglers

in the countryside or in villages and we'd take them. And then more driving, more chasing, more stragglers, more movement. We called it the rat race.

In the meantime, our front was ever widening. We were like a vanguard, a monstrous bird whose wings, once they start expanding, don't stop until the sky is blackened. This widening created more stragglers and prisoners, because our front was cutting German communication lines. Many of the enemy simply didn't know what to do or where to go. So they sat and waited, and many of them were glad to be captured, for German supply lines had also been severed. In some cases the enemy soldiers were not only dirty and bedraggled but hungry as well. Not as hungry as Buchenwald or Leningrad. But hungry.

We had our own no-man's-land at this time, too. The 4th had begun to move so fast that a synapse between us and our infantry was created. That could be very dangerous territory, for just about anyone could turn up there. In fact, George Cardge had quite an experience one day. He was outside the tank, and somehow got separated from the rest of us. Without realizing it, he wound up in no-man's-land, which we called the dead space, or Indian country. Suddenly he saw a German soldier just sitting by the side of the road, his helmet off, his head bowed. George stared at him, incredulously, for a protracted moment or two. Then the German saw Geroge and rose slowly to his feet, his hands on his belt not six inches from his gun.

They stood and stared at each other for another moment or two. Then there was a shot and the German was hurled backward, five yards off the road. George walked quickly to the body and saw a bullet hole in the man's neck. He whirled around to see who had fired the shot. There was no one there. And then, almost as if he were examining a rare species of insect under a magnifying glass, George looked down and saw his own gun in his own hand. But it had stopped smoking.

We moved on. A detachment of 4th Armored ordnancemen

came to a town called Sartilly, with no idea of what it was or who was there. As it turned out, Sartilly was heavily infested with a company of panzers. Fortunately, the Germans simply did not notice any American intrusion. They were like two prowling gunmen who back into each other, whirl around, exclaim their surprise, and start shooting. Now, thanks to some dumb-ass German officer, the ordnancemen got the first lick in, so they wound up sweeping the town in a matter of minutes. It was touchy, however; they were so damn close to catching hell with their pants down and cheeks spread.

They had roared in, in double file, with no effort to disguise or protect their progress. Some of the Americans may have been aware of a hubbub in the rear of the long, cobbled street, but no one had said a word. Suddenly a German officer came running down the road, screaming and gesticulating like a fishwife. A hundred yards away he halted, his eyes widened, and then there was a shot from one of our tanks. The officer crumbled.

Our tanks broke file and started blowing all hell down the street. Sure enough, there was a detachment of Germans trying to assemble some three hundred yards ahead. About fifteen German soldiers were sitting around outside, and they didn't have a chance. In fact, neither did their tanks.

The Americans just didn't stop shooting, not even after every visible enemy tank was aflame. No, you can't come that close to catastrophe (particularly when that catastrophe would have been caused by such an inexcusable slipup on your own part) without overreacting. So they fired and fired and didn't pause for breath. They were blowing out homes and shops. God only knows who they were killing. There were only shadows, the shadows of men and women and pets. And then the shadows would fall, like night in sudden evaporation. But night wasn't evaporating. It was just beginning.

An explanation of the German officer's behavior was eventually passed around. He thought the intruders were Germans, and he was giving them hell for creating a traffic congestion.

That idiot! Stupidity is as unforgivable as premeditated evil. But I suppose all humanity has to eventually rely on the stupidity of its adversaries. How else can a game of chess be won?

Sartilly became famous, a Third Army legend. But I'm glad I missed it.

We moved on. Our next major destination after Avranches was Rennes. As the whole Third Army began to squeeze through Avranches and fan out across Brittany, George Patton began to act like George Patton. It is not difficult to understand him here. After his miseries in Sicily, he felt he had nothing to lose; he could be wild and reckless, and less than assiduous in obeying inhibitive orders from Bradley or Eisenhower. He was up and down the peninsula, jumping into trenches to exhort his men here, shaking his fist and cursing at German planes there. If he were anything less than a man of genius, I'd probably be dead today. Can you imagine being in the hands of an untalented prima donna? Remember Custer?

There was only token resistance blocking the road to Rennes. At times, of course, there was a lot of noise. We'd encounter an occasional camouflaged artillery gun a quarter of a mile ahead. He'd start firing, and we'd send a patrol out to spot him. More often than not, that patrol would spend an hour looking and then return empty-handed; the German gunner, well aware of his vulnerability, would be retreating as he fired. He'd seldom do much damage, but noise is noise. Eventually we or our aerial support would either hit him, or he would fall back and remain silent, waiting for us to pass.

Rennes itself woke us up again. If Avranches was tough for the resistance without the town and the pockets of sneaky resistance within, Rennes was tough for its brutal fortification. This consisted of a ring of artillery, stocked, it seemed, with enough ammunition to last the rest of the war. Rennes provided us our first awful taste of not being able to move forward at all—which, for a division whose very lifeblood was forward movement, was terrifying. In fact, we were actually pushed backward.

I was able to see a space of some one hundred yards of unoccupied ground. Then there was nothing to see. Artillery shells were pummeling us so thoroughly that an absolutely impenetrable smokescreen was set up. You could literally smell the fire burning inside the smoke. To move forward was death. And then the smoke got nearer, and the smell of fire—was it flesh burning? or a tank?—seemed to be chasing me. I saw the tanks around me, about three of them, throw themselves into reverse, and I followed suit.

But as I threw myself backward, I started firing more rapidly, as if I couldn't move backward fast enough to ward off the growing conflagration—and so would shoot it away! Why does anyone shoot faster, more fiercely, when he can't even see the enemy? It was irrational, like flailing your hands in the middle of the Atlantic Ocean in order not to drown—as if you could slap away the ocean. The smoke rose higher and the flames were now visible. A tank had been hit somewhere, and its fuel was igniting the terrain; incoming fire exacerbated it. And I kept falling away, falling away—and firing harder; every time I'd see a billow rise or a flame reach out like a tongue, I'd fire harder. It was irrational all right, but it worked.

It worked because my reaction was hardly unique. Other American tanks were trapped—and *trapped* is the word for it! And those gunners were also firing harder and faster, as irrationally as myself. Our desperate fire, so heightened in intensity by the desperation itself, was scoring, scoring preciously, though we couldn't see the scores for all the smoke. A breeze blew in from somewhere—or was it a breeze? Maybe it was some breath of priceless, fructifying wind reverberating within my own skull. In any case, the smoke grew thinner and dispersed, revealing a plain littered with broken machines and broken men. Now it was a normal battlefield again, a plateau of death punctuated no longer with impenetrable darkness but with the sudden and fierce explosions of artillery shells that had no intention of ceasing. Except now there were fewer of them.

A company of fighting men has a mind of its own; it follows a collective instinct that knows after a few weeks of fire how to swing in appropriate directions with each punch or each opening. And so suddenly I was moving forward again, firing with only slightly less zeal. Now it was the Germans' turn to ward off flame and suffocation. But they threw their cards down and lost the battle. We took Rennes.

Eleven American tanks were lost, the heaviest damage inflicted against the 4th Armored since the beginning. And the outskirts of Rennes looked it. It was very strange, but the skeletons of our tanks were somehow more frightening to me than the torn-up corpses and the occasional arm or leg lying about without an owner. I suppose it was because we were more and more becoming extensions of our machines. Our whole lives were tied in with them. If I were to die, it would probably be in the turret, or I would probably be burned up inside. Yet the thought of being without the tank was like the thought of certain death. They were our cocks and balls. The sight of them devastated, clumped in a heap and leaking oil, was like the aftermath of some grizzly, primitive castration rite, considerably more frightening than a scattered limb.

There was, however, a final, personal satisfaction in the fall of Rennes, which assuaged my tension and gave a more mellow face to my exhaustion. I had helped recapture—from a ruthless band of anti-Semites who possessed unchecked power in their own country—the town in which Alfred Dreyfus had once been tried. There are always private wars to be fought.

The public one would even get better. In a sense, the Germans had thrown so much energy into defending Rennes that now they were in awful trouble. All communications in and out of the city were inoperative. They seemed to be panicking. They were attempting to withdraw in small groups, hoping to avoid the kind of sitting-duck treatment they had received when they fled Avranches. Well, it was a half dozen of one

and six of the other as far as we were concerned! At Avranches the 4th Armored had raced up and down an extended
flank, picking it off at vulnerable points and concentrating on
the rear. Here at Rennes we scouted our prey and picked them
off. In both cases it was our speed that served the purpose. If
your superiority is your ability to cover ground, there's not
much your enemy can do. Either you run up and down his
flank, or you chase him in a thousand zigzagging directions.
We had the capacity for both, and we did both.

Of course, we couldn't take the time to mop up everyone,
not when further progress south and east was the real
premium. Less capable units were given the task of encounter-
ing isolated German forces behind our lines. There would
always be enemy detachments who could consummate their
escape from an Avranches or a Rennes and then hold out
behind us for weeks. When you consider that the 4th was now
stretched out on a fifty-five-mile line through Brittany, with
German mortar ahead of us and individual German units
behind us, you realize that the possibility of a fight at any moment was constant.

We began our move toward Lorient, the 4th Armored's share
of the effort to take the Breton port towns—an effort that
would be abandoned. Not far beyond Rennes a gunner from
another tank, a genuine shmuck that I'll call Anderson, approached me with this sickeningly ingratiating smile on his
face. "Hey Nat, I was about three hundred yards behind you
and those other guys when we were coming up on that town,"
by which he meant Rennes.

"So?"

"So how the hell did you survive?"

How the hell did we survive? No soldier should ever ask
that! How the hell did we survive? They had kings and we had
aces, that's how! That jack-off! But I didn't say a word.

We moved on. I have noted that the German flight from both
Rennes and Avranches had all the earmarkings of a
disorganized, general panic. This, and other factors, have led

many observers to question the real quality of Patton's Brittany campaign. It is true that the enemy was hardly as well trained or as courageous at this time as they would be further south, at the Moselle, in Alsace-Lorraine, and in Germany itself. But who were we? The Third Army was itself a neophyte. Our training was superb, and our valor speaks for itself, but what the Pattons and Woods really accomplished during this period transcended any of our mere potentialities. They actualized us, mobilized and created a body of men with a stunning sense of collective identity. That is as important as any other single element of war.

It may have been a strategic mistake for Patton to have sent a division racing all the way to the coast of France to take Brest. Indeed, it was also a mistake to gear so heavily for Lorient. But once that mistake was perceived as a mistake, he altered the game plan with extreme grace and alacrity. What was wasted at Brest would have been multiplied tenfold had we been in less capable hands.

Historians are also wrong when, in assessing Patton's role, they separate the general as planner from the general as man. Their argument tends to emphasize the mediocrity of strategy during this period, while they simultaneously pay a left-handed compliment to the character who was grabbing off headlines and establishing a name for himself. These observers would say that what was appealing about Patton (at this time, at least) was only his personality; what was lacking, or overrated, was his military acumen. But this misses the point, for the two go together. Patton's personal shenanigans were a vitally important force in the forging of victory. He generated in us a mood of exceptional pugnacity and optimism. He made us feel unique, almost invincible; this inspiration was profoundly coupled with our early experiences at Avranches and Rennes. No, we were not cocky novices who think they can win a war in a week, but wind up with their asses blown off. We were new, to be sure, but we had also been tested in the fire.

Finally, it was during this campaign that Patton formulated

two of the more portentous elements of his whole war philosophy, both of which would find a very enthusiastic supporter and agent in John Wood. First of all, we developed the guerillalike proficiency of aiming for and getting the rear. Second, we cultivated what Patton called the "rock soup method." It's a very cute routine. You reconnoiter, then you reinforce the reconnaissance, then you attack; in other words, a patrol suddenly becomes an army. This is a perfect tactic for a division whose strength is its speed because ever greater effectiveness is gained through ever quicker reinforcement.

Patton had a little story for it. A bum asks for rock soup and it's willingly given him. Then he asks for just a couple of side dishes, like mashed potatoes . . . and asparagus . . . and porterhouse steak. Just side dishes.

Well, these were all formulations from the Brittany campaign, a fact that makes criticism of Patton during this time somewhat mystifying. What we developed here would accelerate in effectiveness throughout the war. If we were invincible in Germany, the seed of that invincibility was planted during the Avranches breakthrough.

We moved on and completely severed the Brittany peninsula. Our progress toward Lorient was enormous; we went seventy miles in seventy hours and came up on Vannes. So even if the initial plan to besiege and take the port towns was a mistake, our celerity and our territorial gains gave that mistake an important, beneficial aspect. And Vannes was one port we had no trouble securing. Once inside, we were afforded a distant glimpse of the Atlantic. The vision of that deep blue, motionless behind the little shops and winding streets, was pure therapy, more settling than the smoothest words of any army psychiatrist or chaplain.

Exemplary air cover from Rennes to Vannes must also be cited; without it our movement would have been impeded by numerous lines of German fire. It was during this seventy-hour period that I first became fully aware of what precision correlation there was between us and XIX Tactical Air Command. The leader of any air support system from TAC was called Yellow Leader; our division ground communication was Egg-cup (hard-boiled, of course). Reconnaissance pickup of resistance was immediately radioed to TAC. Invariably Yellow Leader would wipe out the enemy for us; from Rennes to Vannes he never missed. The planes were mainly Thunderbolts and Mustangs, gorgeous things to look at in formation— all the more gorgeous in that they were seldom more than two hundred yards in front of us.

It was also during this period that the 4th made direct contact with the only French unit I ever respected, the Forces Français de l'Interieur. They were everything the French Resistance was supposed to be but usually wasn't. These soldiers were masters of infiltration. They blew bridges, they sniped officers, they wouldn't let a jeep or truck go by without blowing it. I met one once—a big, bald mother with a broad smile who communicated mostly through affectionately obscene gestures. His English was negligible, and even his French was atrocious. He spoke Breton and fought for Brittany. Hitler could keep Normandy for all he cared.

Indeed, the closer we got to Lorient, the more of a melting pot the war became. Naturally all sorts of German sympathizers could be brought in from the sea and fanned out from the town itself. You never knew who you were liable to run into. They could have had a squadron of Mandingo warriors for all I knew. And yet I was still in for a surprise.

We had to drive about thirty miles west of Vannes in order to ford the Blavet River. Otherwise we simply couldn't have gotten close enough to Lorient. All of the 4th's combat detachments were utilized for this crucial maneuver. On the way there we saw a unit of cavalry on horseback. The horses alone were a little jarring after the big guns of Rennes. Then the word got around. They were Russians!

We moved closer, none of us firing. In fact, we didn't know what the hell to do. Why were they there? Were they supposed to be helping us? Were their stallions going to reinforce our armor? Then the order came to fire. And still we hesitated. I didn't want to be the first to shoot and thereby instigate an international incident with one of our "allies." Who knows, maybe it would cripple the alliance and cost us the eastern front and maybe the war as well.

The order was issued more insistently. Then a pause, and then an explanation. They were goddamn mercenaries! That did it! We wiped them out, and I was glad to see them die. I'm no friend of Karl Marx, let alone Joseph Stalin, but this stunk! All of Leningrad was starving. Every inch of Armenia and the Ukraine was coated with Russian blood, and these bastards were fighting for the Germans! They were probably Ukrainians themselves, for that region was notoriously provincial and no more hostile to Berlin than they were to Moscow.

And yet, even as I relished shooting the men, the slaughter of the horses made me sick. That's a common reaction, and an interesting one. If I were walking down the street and somebody put a gun in my hand and forced me to kill either a passing stranger or an animal, naturally I would, like most people, kill the animal. But war is an affair of men, and it is fought so men can die. Animals are so damn innocent of it all! And that innocence inflates the value of their lives. The same animal whose life you would so casually take in lieu of a human being's becomes, in war, a newborn infant who ought to be safely cradled away somewhere.

Horses also bleed more than men. I can still see the gushers of it. Their riders were beside them, dead or dying, but their human blood was lost in the flood of deep animal red. And I can still see their eyes, those wide, scared, brown circles, eclipsing all the humanity around them. They fell slowly, too slowly, and then their spasms. And then the horses turned and enveloped the soft ground beneath them. I wonder if they listened to Wagner, or read Marx, or had ever been taught to idolize Jefferson or Lincoln or Bismarck or Metternich. And after all the horror of their deaths, I realized with something akin to despair that this butchery of horses had been *the* commonplace of war until 1914. Who hadn't used horses? Who hadn't killed them? Well, that's one thing in favor of technology and technological combat. Machines don't feel pain, and some men deserve it.

Lorient, finally, and a brief siege. Patton's initial desire to take the town was very understandable. Not only were new German recruits and foreign sympathizers or mercenaries brought in via Lorient, but it was also a convenient haven for German U-boats. In fact, even the Japanese had used it for their submarines. Avranches was on the English Channel and therefore less useful, except as a possible point from which to strike at England. But the whole world was in front of Lorient.

The fighting and artillery response around the town was sporadic but very fierce in its active moments. One incident in particular stands out in my mind. I have noted elsewhere that the 4th Armored was responsible for the blowing out of 103 locomotives. I was personally involved in only one such attack. It's quite an experience, derailing and blowing up a train. In a sense, the 4th Armored's outstanding record in this regard supplements our identity as a guerilla-oriented unit, for the sabotage of locomotives is a classic ingredient of most guerilla warfare. God knows, Lawrence of Arabia was adept enough at.it; in every other chapter of *Seven Pillars of Wisdom* somebody is either demolishing a train or expressing a desire to do so.

I suppose that it becomes commonplace for any soldier who does it often enough, but it's cataclysmic the first time, even in the context of an armored siege and heavy artillery retort. The enormous cattle cars separate, they topple in opposite directions, the paneling enflames and smokes, and men spill out like roaches. And then they're helpless. They hurtle out of the burning or motionless or falling cars, and all that is needed is a scatter of fire to unman a company. There must have been sixty guns mopping up the aftermath of the derailment. There were so many Germans falling so easily they barely seemed human. They didn't even have the time to surrender. The ones who survived were the ones who hid behind the fallen box-cars, but even many of them were unfortunate enough to be behind the wrong cars. We were blowing up everything in sight.

It was a memorable moment for yet another, more ambiguous reason. The order to blow up this train had been the second order of the day. The first had been the directive to abandon the siege altogether and move east. We did not know at the time that another division would be picking up the siege, nor did we realize exactly how important Lorient was and how strategically necessary it would be to harass the city as much as possible. We thought we were simply leaving it alone. Every one of our gunners, who wreaked such hell on that train and the men within it, consequently thought that this slaughter was purely gratuitous. I know I did. I believed at the time that we were destroying for the simple sake of destroying, and I remember having to fall back on all the clichéd rationalizations in the world to keep from thinking of myself as a total animal. All command decisions are lonely, but some ought to be explained. Wood's failure to do so, and the potentially demoralizing effect this failure could have had, was certainly his worst—perhaps his only—mistake in the war.

We moved on. It was eastward this time, a course we would maintain until the Battle of Singling. Units of the 4th used seven hours to reach Nantes, and they cleared it. From what I'm told, it had been a very idyllic town before the war, and now it has returned to that state. Beyond Nantes was Orléans, the town where a young schizophrenic virgin had once heard voices. Those voices, which were the voices of angels, sang of cold steel, English villainy, and the atrocities of a war that would last over one hundred years. Those angels were gone, quite gone, by 1944; divisions of Germans were there instead, and the ironclad monsters that drove the Germans out came from a heaven Joan could never have guessed at or understood. There were no voices in George Patton's heaven; only trumpets.

The 4th attacked Orléans from the north and from the east. Beyond, to the south, was the Loire. A successful attack would trap the enemy at the river. Tactics, tactics. Units of the 4th had backtracked to La Loupe to plug up the Falaise Gap. Other 4th detachments had gone to Sens to gain access across the Yonne River. Then they regrouped and charged Orléans.

The whole tactic exemplifies the genius of the division itself. Had either task force slowed down or been turned aside, Orléans might have become a real impediment. But the units at the Falaise weren't about to lose any time; firing with savage rapidity and force, they scattered the German congregations. And the other units hit Sens so fast, the occupying Germans didn't even have time to get off the streets. Sens was taken with only seven Americans wounded.

Then Orléans itself, the consummation of a perfect tactic. The Germans had nowhere to go but south, and then—what do you know—a river! Our guns zeroed in. It was like battering an infant. Many of the Germans were running *toward* us as fast as they could, hoping to cheat death by surrendering. Many of them made it. The others were burned at the stake, but no pope would canonize them.

Beyond Orléans rivers were falling to the 4th as if by the dozen—the same rivers that had posed such knotty tactical problems to the militarists of preindustrial centuries. Units of the 4th took Courtenay, then Montargis. It was like gathering sand in your fist. And Paris. Paris was outflanked.

And we moved on, exploiting every opportunity our progress afforded us. In the fiercest fight I had known since Rennes, we secured access across the Seine at Troyes. It was still August—August 25, 1944. Patton was still a new commander, and we were still new. But what a long month. Worlds, universes, clusters of universes, had been created and destroyed in the interval of time it took late July to become late August.

It was wholly unique, this battle at Troyes. Our orders had called for a direct frontal assault to secure the town. Wood had measured probable enemy resistance and estimated the nimblest and most efficient method of following up victory with a bridgehead across the river; the results of his calculations suggested this solid, simple approach. The only hitch was a slight error on the part of reconnaissance in reporting the strength of the German forces. We went in expecting five hundred enemies; we encountered two thousand.

There were now no real advantages on either side. It was simply an old-fashioned face-off. We were adept at this sort of frontal assault because we had trained in it almost exclusively at Ibis. In fact, the exact wording of the order had called for "desert formation." We were merely bringing the desert to the vinyards of northern France. And we moved as fast toward the waiting enemy as if we were simply racing across a road and swallowing uncontested geography. There were ditches everywhere that we were literally jumping. It must have been quite a picture from above. A division of tanks barrels across wet soil as if it were the Sahara, almost rockets upward every time a ditch threatens to impede it—and, maybe a mile away, two thousand heavy-duty Germans wait to use their bayonets if necessary.

It never came to bayonets, though I remember one American who might as well have been impaled. His intestines were oozing out, slowly, greasily; then a burst of shrapnel ripped up his face and he fell, writhing—losing, it seemed, his entire organic content. He looked like Zasu Pitts without the pits.

We lit up Troyes with phosphorescent shells, infiltrating every corner of it. But simply obliterating the town wouldn't help. We needed the ground itself, not the town, for our real objective was the river. And the Germans fought better than at any time I had seen in Brittany. They were out for blood. We pushed them back and reached the outer perimeter of the town. It was there that I saw two American medics scrambling over our wounded. Then I saw a half dozen or so German guns some five hundred yards away aim for the noncombatants. Others saw it too—for not only was the story passed around at length after the battle, but I distinctly remember at least five 4th Armored guns, including my own, aim for the distant killers. We got at least two, while the others fell back. But it was too late; the medics were stretched out dead on cobblestone. The herons had found their fish, and the blood was still dripping down their narrow beaks.

The tide of the battle probably turned when we started scoring German ammunition trucks. I don't know how many got through, but we blew out a dozen at least. There were explosions everywere, like geysers of fire shooting up and out with rapine impulsiveness. The enemy fell back faster now, unsure how they could possibly maintain a forceful counterfire. When night fell, the center of Troyes was ours.

Our infantry was brilliant. From the time we took the center of town to the last horror of the German evacuation, I was not fired upon by a single bazooka. They were gunned, grenaded, sniped; our men could have been kicking them to death for all I knew. The Germans retreated east, where a detachment of our tanks was waiting. And then a line of Thunderbolts finished the job. Over five hundred Germans died. Over five hundred were captured.

And after the battle was over, something struck me, something I had not bothered to realize in the midst of the heavy fighting. Those had not been regular German soldiers defending Troyes; they were SS troops. No wonder those two medics had been murdered!

We moved on; we all moved on. The 4th crossed the Marne with, again, consummate tactical skill. Creighton Abrams took his 37th across at the north and successfully attacked the

German stronghold at Châlons-sur-Marne. The higher plateaus around the river were taken and crossed by an equally strong 4th Armored detachment, Task Force Jaques (named after its leader from the 53rd), which also seized the town of Vitry.

We consolidated our gains in Saint-Dizier, which the 4th took in a quick, bloody fight, and in the woods between the Seine and the Aube, which were completely cleared. And it was still August! We were still supposed to be babies. Well, these babies were becoming famous. We had crossed almost all of northern France, and we gazed, teddy bears and rattles in hand, we gazed toward Berlin.

Ahead of us lay the Meuse and the Moselle. Even though we had already crossed so many rivers and streams, these two merit a separate chapter. What distinguishes them is not merely the haunting resonance of World War I; they provide, in addition, a convenient historical division, for beyond them lay the second third of our journey, which would take us from Alsace-Lorraine up to the Battle of the Bulge. And the last leg would carry us through Germany and propel us to legend.

# 3

# The Warrior God

Ten seconds . . .

I saw George Patton, the Third Army's boss, bully, lover, and godfather, on two occasions. On one of those occasions I had actual personal contact with this man, and it lasted ten seconds, that's all. And yet the memory of those ten seconds continues to haunt my life as if it had been a thousand years. I could have been married to the goddamn guy, that's how forceful the encounter was and that's how persistent its memory.

Do you remember the scene in the George C. Scott movie in which Patton himself is directing tanks, and screams bloody murder at one that's gotten itself bogged down? It's a tribute to the research behind that movie that even that small incident was real and was portrayed accurately. I know because that was my tank, and I was in the turret at the time.

Let's skip ahead a bit, to the end of 1944. We were on our way to Bastogne, having just gotten the order to beat it north and rescue the First Army. Patton himself wasn't sure what it was all about. Bradley had given him the order over the phone, and when Patton protested that with a little rest his men could zoom in on Germany itself, Bradley cut him short and said that

39

he couldn't talk about it on the phone. This was the Battle of the Bulge, Hitler's trump card and, strategically, the crucial moment of the European war.

No one could have convinced the men of the 4th Armored that such a crucial confrontation was in the works. After all, we had just linked up with Alexander Patch's Seventh Army at the Belfort Gap, and no one, not even the bloodiest and craziest of us, would imagine that any fight could be more hard won and, therefore, more important. How could we know that Hitler's whole attitude toward our linkup was almost desultory, that his real trick lay elsewhere? And how could we know that future historians would just about forget that there ever was a struggle for the Belfort Gap?

The point is, we were exhausted—as if we had been singled out for apocalypse. The road to Bastogne was simply more apocalypse, simply more of what we thought we couldn't see and wouldn't see. There was no stable line. We were inside a folding accordion, expanding and contracting, hissing and sputtering. In any combat situation the absence of a stable line makes for snipers, and we had them in our soup. They're doing their job, but you can't help but hate them. You never know when they'll hit. I saw one guy get it in the head while he was dipping a piece of biscuit in his gruel. I saw another guy take it in the neck while he was laughing at somebody's joke. He died with the laughter glued to his face.

In fact, my first kill was a sniper. It was a long time before the run to Bastogne, but I kept thinking about it now as we fended off other snipers. I had been in my turret when somebody yelled to me to back my tank up. I did so, and a man pointed up at a tree to my left. I ordered my gunner to lay off; as I say, you can learn to hate snipers, and this one I wanted. I took a .30-caliber machine gun—what was called a coaxial— and I blew him down. Then I pinned his corpse on the road and shot it along for fifty yards. Finally, someone grabbed me and shouted, "What the hell, Frankel, you want Swiss cheese for lunch?"

Anyway, months and months later, we were pushing ourselves ever nearer to Bastogne. And, as I said, we were tired, shot up, and our maintenance status was a god-awful mess. We had been rolling so fast that my tank had never been properly tended to. I bogged down in the mud, and, perplexed and frustrated, I stuck my head out the turret. I looked around and who did I see?

The first thing I saw was those two damn guns of his. Ivory-handled—ivory, not pearl, for, as he himself so famously said, only St. Louis pimps wear pearl-tipped guns. They were strapped across his hips like a portable totem pole. Then I saw his eyes, glowering like two jewels planted in a Polynesian idol. In fact, I can't walk by a Trader Vic or Kon-Tiki restaurant without thinking of that goddamn general.

His arms were waving, randomly but not frantically. He was the very picture of total energy combined with godlike self-control. I knew it was Patton, but I didn't think: That's George Patton, a man with a body and mind just like mine; a man who worries, loves, shits, and pisses just like me. For the duration of our encounter, for that unreal ten seconds, he was barely human. It was like my tank had run up against a mountain. And in that mountain there was a gorge, and out of that yawning abyss words came forth; there was a god in the mountain, and when he spoke, the whole valley trembled.

"What's wrong?" he bellowed.

I told him.

"Goddamn! This is no time to get stuck! Get this goddamn thing rolling!"

Now, I didn't take this lying down. I answered him. I answered him loudly, intrepidly, clearly. No, Nat Frankel isn't a man to hesitate or cower. But I'm not going to tell you what I said, not for a while anyway. Before I do, not only do I feel compelled but—in the interests of any man who ever fought and bled anonymously for the greater glory of another man, Alexander or Caesar or Patton—I feel obliged to explore the contours of the warrior god's personality. How much do *I* know? What can *I* say? I have my intuitions, and why should they be any less significant than the dutiful tributes of a Ladislas Farago or the purely professional analyses of a Charles Whiting?

When I think of George Patton, I think of a huge rock cut and angled in numerous directions. You can't tell its real shape, not even when you turn it around a half-dozen times. Least of all can you pick it up and pocket it neatly. There is, first of all, little doubt that George Patton and Erwin Rommel were the two greatest military geniuses of the twentieth century at least—and the fact that they faced each other renders the war with Germany all the more portentous. Patton's greatness was not something we figured out in 1946. We knew it before Bastogne, and everyone in the Third Army knew it. And yet we had mixed feelings about him. We didn't love him like we loved General Wood or Creighton Abrams. We took Patton's grandstanding with a grain of salt. In fact, there was an expression floating around the Third Army whenever Patton's nickname, Old Blood and Guts, was mentioned. We'd say, "Yeah, our blood and his guts."

Yet what is so telling is the fact that we *knew* that he was playing up to an image, yet we respected both him and the image at the same time. It was, after all, a stunning image, and there must have been something real underneath it that enabled him to play it so well. Trying to live up to an image is also a dangerous thing because if you set yourself up like that, the least chink in the armor will bring you down in a very demeaning fall. History is full of men whose grandstanding, whose ability to inspire reverence, ended in catastrophe once the least human failing was glimpsed. I think of Mark Antony and Daniel Webster and Lyndon Johnson.

And yet we saw those chinks in Patton too: the slapping incident, his fallibility at the Moselle, and the stupid and selfish attack on Hammelburg, which warrants a later chapter. We saw the chinks in him, yet he never fell. It may be that there was enough of the acutal stuff in him, the real blood and guts, to override evidence of his normal humanity. But I think it was also because we needed to be led by a George Patton. We needed to believe so badly that the fact that he was at all times playing some sort of a game with himself and with us didn't ultimately matter. It's what's called a willing suspension of disbelief.

So were we inspired by him, inspired in the old sense that he was a noble general astride a white horse leading a collection of insignificant humanity to hell and extinction? We were—we were indeed—but it was no naïve allegiance to a childish fantasy. We knew he was a bastard, but we were moved by the grandeur, not to mention the fear, his presence generated— and we respected the extraordinary lengths to which he was willing to go to maintain and promulgate his own image. I suppose that it takes as much energy, if nothing else, to be George Patton as it does to confront any enemy in any combat situation. Most people like to sit back, relax, scratch their bellies, and bullshit. When you're George Patton, you can't do that— not with your men, not with your friends, maybe not even with your wife. His commitment to his ideal was gigantic, however perverse the ideal. And one person's giant commitments tend to inspire the same in others around him, despite their own continuing realization that it's basically all a lot of crap.

For me, the issue was even more complicated. This is nothing that I can document, but it was commonly assumed—at least among the soldiers—that George Patton hated Jews. Despite the fact that I've known some Jews who could beat all shit out of a platoon (remember Benny Leonard? or Benny Siegel?), we are not known as a race that is given to displays of physical prowess or violence. Patton probably saw us as a cringing people, surviving through stealth, using our brains to scheme up ideas to save ourselves and fuck others. In other words, Patton was probably a prototypical anti-Semite.

Who, then, was the enemy, and why? Hitler was not merely the enemy of my country, but a personal enemy of both my forebears and my children. It was not, of course, difficult for me to rationalize shooting either him or his enforcers. But the agonizing paradox was that I was being led to do so by a man who probably shared some of his opinions. No doubt I personally would have felt more comfortable with Rommel. Of course there's nothing historically new about a soldier like Patton having something in common with the enemy. Sherman, for example, believed in slavery. But how would I have felt being a freed slave in Sherman's army? Well, I know how I would have felt: the same way I felt being Jewish under Patton.

I remember talking after the war with a Jewish infantry sergeant who had not served in the Third Army. I shared some of my complicated thoughts about Patton with him, and he told me a priceless story. It was his duty as a noncom to go out on patrol every day—every single goddamn day! That's like sticking your head in a lion's mouth on Monday, not feeding him all day, then repeating your act on Tuesday. But it was his job, and since we try to be as fair as possible, we pick different soldiers to go with us on different days.

Now this sergeant did not have a name like Goldberg or Berkowitz; it was, in fact, a name that sounded purely Polish. One day, he and a few men were out on patrol and they got pinned down. Two of them died at once. They shot back enough volleys to force a surcease, but they couldn't move. The Germans were just waiting, probably for a surrender. During this hiatus a private turns to the Jewish sergeant with the Polish name.

"I'll tell ya', Sarge, do you know where I'd like to be now?"

"Where?"

"Where the Jews are! Fucking Jews, man, sitting on their fucking asses, rolling bills, while you and me are taking all this heat!"

"Yeah?"

"Hell, yes! We ought to be shooting them, too!"

"Yeah?"

The Germans opened up again, and the patrol fired back. My friend ordered his boys to fire continuously while they circled to the right. It was a good move because the enemy couldn't maneuver themselves fast enough. So four or five Germans fell, and the patrol made it back. Now they were in camp, and my friend confronted the Jew hater.

"I'm going to do you a favor, boy. You want to be where the Jews are? I'll see to it that you will be. All the time. In fact, boy, you're going to spend the rest of your life where the Jews are. I'm a Jew, and I'm not going out on patrol again without you."

The kid fell to his knees and begged my friend. He pulled out his wallet and showed him a picture of his girlfriend and one of his parents. No dice. He went out on patrol every day that week, except Saturday. He had his head blown off on Friday.

"So you see, Nat," my friend said to me. "I had to decide who the enemy was."

Was Patton my enemy? Well, in one sense, he had to be. I couldn't love him, and yet I couldn't resist the force of his personality. Though he hated me, I knew he could lead me to the destruction of a man whose hatred was more fundamental and more dangerous. And again I would point to that nearly maniacal energy of his, that grandiose commitment that swept a whole army along with it. What was the source of that energy? How could any man feel such a monumental commitment, not to a cause but to an image that is fleeting, chimerical, possibly unreal even to the man himself?

I can't pinpoint an answer to that immediately, but I can move toward an understanding of Patton by comparing his personality with that of four others. Maybe we can see Patton by drawing his outline, by separating him from other types of figures around him.

Take Doug MacArthur, for example. Good old Doug. You've seen pictures of him, his hands on his hips, his head thrown back, that white scarf flowing down around his neck. He's standing on a beach, a riding crop by his side, his sunglasses glinting in the lucid air. He's standing on a beach, and you can be sure the nearest Jap is two or three thousand miles away!

And notice the same pose in Herbert Hoover's day: good old Doug, reconnoitering the war-torn environs. Except this time it isn't the Philippines, it's Pennsylvania Avenue, and the enemy is the bonus marcher: starving, defenseless veterans of World War I. That prick! George Patton would be no more capable of attacking unarmed veterans than he would be of sticking his own head in a feculent toilet bowl. Patton's unrelenting sense of honor made him difficult, fierce, sometimes stupid—but it was honor nonetheless. He was innately incapable of relating to politics. He despised politics! MacArthur, meanwhile, thought of very little else but politics. His whole life was aimed toward nothing else but a shot at the presidency, toward a challenge to Harry Truman—and what an effective challenge it turned out to be! Fortunately the Republicans, wooing Ike, wanted no part of him in 1952.

MacArthur no doubt grew up playing with toy boats in his bathtub. Slowly his fantasies of triumph began to take shape, to assume the lineaments of real possibility. And what would be the climax of his fantasy? Why, the people would lift him atop their shoulders and gratefully carry him to the seat of absolute power. Patton probably had similar fantasies as a child, but with a crucial difference. Here there is fantasy and glory and triumph, but glory for its own sake. No populace would carry Patton to his coronation or apotheosis. For Patton the glories of war would be their own reward, and life itself would end when war would end.

Patton and MacArthur: two very different minds craving two different varieties of glory. And yet to understand Patton, we have to contrast him not only to a contemptible fraud like MacArthur but to a superior sort of warrior as well. That way we can see a larger perspective. And who would that superior warrior be? Our deadly enemy, Erwin Rommel!

What made Rommel tick? In a sense, it was something even more anachronistic than the love of glory. It was the love of duty. I remember speaking to a German veteran of World War I who went to school with Rommel in Freiburg. He remembers him as quiet and unassuming, but totally dependable, unimpeachable in behavior or discipline. He even sat like a German, his back rigid against the uncomfortable wooden chair backs. And yet this was no robotlike duty. It was based on a sense of obligation to society, to Germany, and to whatever fraction of human interest Germany represented. But when Hitler led Germany further on the road to senseless destruction, Rommel reinterpreted that same discipline that my friend had noticed in Freiburg—reinterpreted it to the extent of trying to kill Hitler and losing his own life in the process.

So Rommel, growing up with no more fantasy than total commitment to personal responsibility, became the desert fox, the most glorious of soldiers. Yet it was not a mantle he openly sought or sued for. It was given him by the German propaganda machine during the war, and by admiring Englishmen afterward. Once he received it, he simply continued to do what he had been doing: fight a war as adequately as he knew how. Had Rommel been running Germany, an American defeat in World War II would not have been too terribly tragic. But, of course, had Rommel been running Germany, there probably wouldn't have been a World War II. Unlike Patton, Rommel didn't revel in it.

Yet all we've seen so far is the difference between three warrior-mandarins, three different types of self-image operating in men who sent hordes of innocent soldiers to an ambiguous death. But what was the actual force operating in Patton that so compelled him to make childhood fantasy become adult reality? I mean, I've had fantasies too. You know, conquering the Spanish Armada, having an affair with Queen Elizabeth, mowing down the Turks, getting myself canonized by a grateful pope whose domain I've rescued from the bar-

barians. But believe it or not, when I go through an average day, driving a cab or picking up a woman, I don't actually think of myself as or behave like Essex or Julius Caesar or Alexander Nevski. But Patton did. Why?

Well, take Pop Cronan or Ernie Jacobson. Who, you may well ask, are Pop Cronan and Ernie Jacobson? After the heady company of Patton, MacArthur, and Rommel, I am somewhat relieved to tell you that Cronan and Jacobson were dog soldiers attached to the 4th Armored. Cronan was a mechanic, Jacobson a gunner. Cronan grew up somewhere in Georgia. Probably dirt poor. I know he was illiterate. Probably saw life and death as a regular portion of his existence: animals bleating their life away, or redneck women giving birth in an open field, or drunken hillbillies slicing each other up on a Saturday night.

He probably left home when he was thirteen or fourteen. Why stick around? For what? His whole life was the bottom of the barrel. There was no television, so he didn't even know what the top of the barrel looked like. He lived in hobo jungles and back streets; he slept only with whores. And did a lot of running, for Pop wasn't a violent sort by nature; he had only been seeing it all his life.

Then came official violence, the virtuous variety. Tojo hit Pearl Harbor, and Pop enlisted. The army taught him how to fix a motor and retread a tank. He wasn't looking for glory. What meaning could glory possibly have for such a man? The same violence that to a commander-in-chief was the stuff of dreams, childhood dreams, was to Cronan the same old sordid shit. Oh, and Pop needed his own dreams, which had nothing to do with Alexander the Great and everything to do with the bottom of a bottle. That was *his* destination. For Patton fate was the bombed-out streets of Berlin. For Cronan it was the round and barren bottom of a shot glass.

Or take Ernie Jacobson, a gunner. I know where he was from: a section of New York I don't even like to walk through.

Known far and wide as Hell's Kitchen, it has produced more gangsters, mainly Irish and Jews, than Little Italy. Ernie was a heavy. I liked him in Europe, but I don't think I would have wanted him collecting interest payments from me on the West Side docks. He knew war before he got to Europe. He knew what happens when the same territorial lust that moves the Hitlers and Stalins, the Roosevelts and Churchills, moves Dutch Schultz to assume control of the policy racket in Harlem. When negotiations broke down between Cordell Hull and the Japanese, we had a war. Ernie knew all about it because when "negotiations" broke down between Lucky Luciano and Benny Siegel, there was also a war. It didn't last five years, but blood is blood.

So what sort of fantasies did Ernie bring with him to Europe? Of course, he didn't bring any! He had none, or at least he had fewer than did a man like myself. And my fantasies I left in Queens. Only Patton brought his with him.

Instead of the backwoods of Georgia, or the back allies of Hell's Kitchen, George Patton was raised on the outskirts of Pasadena. He, and ten thousand little old ladies! Cronan and Jacobson had a very substantial notion of reality coming in; they had no illusions. But what could life have taught Patton beyond the reverberations of his own lonely skull? His background was nondescript. So is the land from which he came. It is not a land which can teach you much of anything. In the anonymous, dull terrain of Pasadena people are left to their own lonesome devices. Whatever the mind of the child thinks becomes reality. Whatever the adolescent does shapes his life. It's a weird kind of freedom.

In a sense, there's no such thing as the present in Pasadena. The present is a vacuum. There are four walls around you and green grass outside; unassuming, almost invisible people talk their small talk around you. There's no hillbilly with a knife, no gangster overlord reciting the syllables of day-to-day reality. So you do more than fall back on yourself. You fall back on the past and the future. But mainly the past, for the mighty dead live in the past and so do their valorous deeds. You erase yourself and fall back totally on them.

Which is precisely what George Patton did. The man, after all, believed in reincarnation. He believed that the present is nothing more than the theater in which the giants of the past repeat their mighty deeds. In fact, Patton didn't even believe in people. He believed only in deeds.

And, of course, he himself was no blacksmith trailing behind Alexander's army. Oh no, he was Alexander himself. Quite literally. Not "I am like Alexander." Not "My deeds are the same deeds as Alexander's." No. "I AM ALEXANDER!" Read his poem "Through a Glass Darkly." It was Patton who crossed the Alps with a million elephants. They just called him something different then. And it was Patton who held a narrow pass, saving Greece from the Persians. And it was Patton who also fought *against* Hannibal. And it was Patton who conquered Mesopotamia for Cyrus. It's all the same man—or, rather, no man at all, just one enormous deed resounding through history.

So this was the loon who controlled our lives. But who am I to say he wasn't actually Alexander or Hannibal, reincarnated to fight the Hun? (Notice, too, the atavistic way in which Patton always called the Germans the Hun.) Considering the way he thought, you can imagine his problems! Imagine being the reincarnation of Alexander the Great and having to play politics with Eisenhower and Montgomery! Imagine having to play politics with anyone! In fact, the whole notion of alliance with other nation states must have secretly gnawed away at him. The nation state, after all, was a contrivance of renaissance merchants. This modern exigency could only cramp the style of a mythical warrior. Alexander the Great may have invented modern strategy, but can you imagine him coordinating his operations with some foreign potentate, whose skill and acumen he would have to rely on? The idea would have been as repugnant to Alexander as it was to Patton.

And you can see how his belief that he was Alexander and Hannibal colored all his attitudes. When he perceived fallibility in himself, how overwhelming that must have been! For to admit that he was only human would have done more than shatter his personal self-image. It would have shaken his whole universe; it would have dislodged and demeaned Caesar and Hannibal and Robert E. Lee. For Patton to admit to himself that he was only human would have destroyed all the glorious work of all the glorious centuries!

Or even worse. Imagine Patton's thoughts when Ike put him on ice or subordinated him to Bradley. How could these small petty concerns actually be allowed to degrade forty centuries of valor? How could the world reject the presence of the great master who had returned to despoil and re-create? What kind of a world was this?

Worse yet. He had managed to win the war, and what did the Philistines force on Alexander the Great? He had to befriend the Russians! Here we had a people, or an ideology, that didn't even believe in individual glory but placed all of its faith in the blind, dehumanizing force of the collective mass. And we were supposed to kiss their asses? Why, it was the end of the world!

And what a world Patton foresaw coming! A world in which war was wholly mechanized, in which a button replaced the soul of the soldier. No glory at all. The death of the great fantasy! So you can imagine, then, how incredibly prepossessing Patton's notion of himself must have been. He wasn't merely Alexander the Great. He was the *last* Alexander the Great, the monumental hero facing the final twilight.

But Patton had his glory, his taste of that vintage Caesar drank after crossing the Rubicon—which, after all, was due to Patton, since he *was* Caesar. The glory came after he crossed the Rhine. Observers have noted that at that point, Hammelburg notwithstanding, Patton thought he was infallible. How could he be anything else but infallible? A man is only subject to error when he himself has freedom of choice. But

Patton had none. All that was involved was for him to wake up in the morning and do the things destiny had decreed Alexander should do in the final hours of the heroic cycle.

So Patton wakes up in the morning. He brushes his teeth and takes a crap. He puts his uniform on. Then, a staff meeting. Impatience bristles in every corner of his face. How can they not see? . . . Don't they realize? . . . Sounds of shells, real and imagined, pursue him throughout the day. Each one of his thoughts is a small step toward a major moment: his own deification, his own proof that he is Alexander. Soldiers pass him in corridors, on the streets. A respectful fear passes across their faces. Well, that's the way it should be! Every moment is weighted. He eats dinner, feasting on duck or beef. The night falls, and he goes to bed amid all the superhuman shadows of history. And if he dreams, he dreams mere human dreams and so forgets them quickly.

That same day Douglas MacArthur wakes up somewhere in the Pacific. He knows that someday he'll be in Japan, if only because an island with no sea superiority cannot maintain superior world power for too long. But maybe today is the day Iwo Jima is won. Ira Hayes raises the flag and sets another jewel in MacArthur's crown. MacArthur closes his eyes and foresees a day when congressmen and governors will weaken, when an America terrified by the specters of Mao and Lenin will have only him to turn to. He washes his face that night, goes to bed, and dreams of this future day, and of this future day only.

Erwin Rommel is awakened in the night by another communiqué from Hitler. Do not retreat one inch. Die if necessary. Is the man mad? He can't be reasoned with! Rommel crawls out of bed, brushes his teeth, and washes his face. He doesn't know what to do. He doesn't know what to do because he can no longer comprehend the dimensions of his own duty. Is it merely the responsibility to win a war? Is it obedience to Hitler's commands? Or does he have a higher duty? He doesn't know, and every waking moment is obsessed by his doubt. He speaks to subordinates, jokes with friends, tries to pick up the morale of his sagging army. But he's only half there. His mind is elsewhere, preoccupied. He goes to bed that night and tries not to dream at all.

Pop Cronan wakes up at six A.M. and doesn't bother to wash his face or brush his teeth. First on the agenda is the captain's jeep; its tire is flat. He squats by the side of the vehicle and good-naturedly fields joking obscenities from familiar passers-by. By ten A.M., someone has sold him a bottle of gin, which he drinks away by noon. At two, he's doing his best with the motor of a tank. By seven he's gotten into some wine. When he goes to sleep, he dreams the same dream he's been dreaming all day.

Ernie Jacobson has been gunning his way to Bastogne. He's probably killed fifty or sixty men in Europe. Maybe more in the United States, who knows? But the brass likes him, and why not? Nothing goes to his head. Today, as always, he's cool and friendly; he shares his cigarettes. Except today a shell hits Ernie's tank and blows it and its gunner from hell to breakfast. And now Ernie will dream the same dreams that all dead men dream.

Not Cronan. Not Jacobson, either. I don't know his name, the soldier that Patton slapped. Why would he do such a thing? How could one man, in the context of an army hospital—not, mind you, in the crucial hours of combat—so quickly, so impulsively, and yet so self-assuredly judge and condemn another man's hysterics?

"I'll not have him in the same room with brave men," Patton had screamed.

What kind of nonsense was this? Who did this bastard-killer think he was? Well, we've already shown who he thought he was, and therein lies the key to the whole notorious slapping incident.

It wasn't so much that Patton was offended by a "coward" contaminating the other soldiers. I think, rather, that at that moment the "reincarnated" Patton had the upper hand. Fantasy had taken over. Things had to go in a certain way for Alexander the Great. Soldiers didn't cry in a child's picture book of historical greats. If they did, they offended as much as did a demand to play politics with Montgomery; they were as disturbing to the natural order of things as a request to treat Russian generals with extreme deference.

So Patton struck the soldier on behalf of his military picture books and the great men remembered therein. There was, however, another World War II picture book, which taunted and debunked Patton's own. I'm talking about the drawings of Bill Mauldin, later collected as *Up Front*. No Alexander the Greats in that one. And we all know what Patton thought of Bill Mauldin.

In fact, Patton personally took the complaint to Ike. He threw the Joe and Willie cartoons in front of Ike's face as if he were an irate prosecutor displaying porno pictures to a judge. Now Ike, the great political genius of World War II, was nothing if not realistic: realistic enough to know that Joe and Willie had a lot more to do with World War II than the weird fantasies of George Patton. So when Patton complained to Ike, what did Ike do?

He laughed at Patton. Ouch!

Now I have dealt at length with our respect, however grudging, for Patton and of his ability, however qualified, to inspire us, if only by the demonic energy with which he adhered to his own image. And yet I am what I am, and I suppose I'll take Bill Mauldin any day. In fact, there is one cartoon by Mauldin— whom I never met but who spent more than a little time with the 4th Armored—that I can't help but think of when I think of Patton.

Joe and Willie are in a trench, their guns peeking out over the top. Some young stalwart officer is standing atop the trench, his eyes steadfastly gazing upward and outward. Joe looks up and says, "Excuse me, lootenant, but do you think you can try to inspire us without drawing fire?"

But of course the main image I have of Patton is of that man waving his arms angrily at me as we pushed our way toward Bastogne and Hitler's death knell. I must have been hoping for the best when I stared down at that mountain, roaring to me to get my machine going. But, as I have said, I was man enough for the occasion. I said the only tough and intelligent and sensible thing that a man can say to George Patton at such a time.

I said, "YESSIR!"

Deeds, not people. Deeds. "By their deeds and their deeds alone shall you know them," John Wood said of us, but that could have been Patton talking. What phalanx were we? From where did Patton remember us? Gaul? Philippi? Austerlitz? If he knew that he was Alexander and Napoleon, he knew something else as well: the fact that no Caesar can do great deeds alone. Without Mickey Mantle and Whitey Ford, Casey Stengel is a lonely man on a lonely mountain.

So we were part of his fantasy. Isn't all war a kind of fantasy? It is something too catastrophic to be comprehended with the daily currencies of the sane mind. So, given the fact of war, given its surreal horror, who can judge George Patton? Extraordinary circumstances call for extraordinary beings.

We would have won the war without him, but something would have been lost. We would have pushed our way to Berlin, impelled by small men, with small fantasies, simply protecting their own small careers. I wasn't ready to die for Patton's fantasies, but, in an odd way, the fact of his madness— and I don't hesitate to call it that—dignified the madness of combat. I would, for example, rather be destroyed by the delusions of a godlike maniac than be brutalized into oblivion by the petty machinations of a bureaucrat.

I remember a young soldier, an infantryman, whom I met during the fight for Metz. God, how he hated Patton's guts! This man, who was something of a leftist and certainly an intellectual, would often comment on the shame of dying for someone else's lust for glory. At this time there was some competition between the Third and First Armies regarding the German defense at the West Wall and the crossing of the Moselle. I remember him sitting over a drink one night and estimating the number of lives that would be saved if strategy could be coordinated by less self-seeking men. Five thousand here. Ten thousand there.

Then someone else spoke up. "If Patton weren't such a fuck, we'd be moving much slower. And that would cost more lives."

"All you're saying," the Patton hater answered, "is that we're damned if we do and damned if we don't."

The other man shrugged his shoulders. I don't think he really cared enough to get into an argument over facts of life he couldn't change anyway.

But then the Patton hater said a remarkably interesting thing. "Well, at least I know what it's like to fight for Napoleon." It is only now, as I reflect upon Patton, that I realize how significant that remark was. Here was a man who loathed George Patton but nonetheless comprehended the warrior god in the warrior god's own terms.

And believe me, as the Third Reich began to crumble like dust, as millions of human lives all over the world were evaporated in blasts of steel and smoke, there were very few other terms capable of making any kind of sense.

And don't jump to the assumption that the anticlimactic nature of Patton's death eradicated or even qualified those lofty terms. About twenty-five hundred years ago Patton, a Macedonian conqueror, contracted pneumonia in Persia, leaving his empire "to the strongest." And a few hundred years later Patton, the first Roman emperor, was stabbed to death by his best friend and a bunch of ambitious politicians. Eighteen hundred years later Patton, a Corsican corporal who conquered most of Europe, died, maybe poisoned, on a small and desolate island in the Atlantic. The Patton I knew died in a jeep but, like all the others, had his share of glory.

A tank crew at Pine Camp, late 1941.

Training maneuver in the Mojave, early 1943.

The 80th Tank Battalion—Camp Bowie, Texas.

Normandy—what we found when we landed, July 1944. *Photograph by Robert Capa/Magnum Photos, Inc.*

The lap of Norman luxury, July 1944. Photograph by Robert Capa/Magnum Photos, Inc.

Guarding prisoners just outside St. Lô, early August 1944.
*Photograph by Robert Capa/Magnum Photos, Inc.*

German prisoners—a common sight in Brittany.
*Photograph by Robert Capa/Magnum Photos, Inc.*

The 4th Armored crosses the Meuse, early September 1944.

Infantrymen cross the Moselle, September 12, 1944.
*U.S. Army Photograph.*

Our engineers build a pontoon across the Moselle, September 12, 1944.
*U.S. Army Photograph.*

A new M-4 A-3 with 76mm gun equipped with muzzle brake, covers
highway H-4 near Bastogne. *U.S. Army Photograph.*

The V- for victory haircuts that would terrify the Germans.

Pillboxes, somewhere between Arracourt and Metz, November 1944.

Strafing the Moselle during the approach to Metz, October 6, 1944.
*U.S. Army Photograph.*

One of our tanks bogged down in the cold mud of Singling, December 1944.

Infantrymen trek toward Bastogne, around December 20, 1944.
Photograph by Robert Capa/Magnum Photos, Inc.

Tank deployment in the Bulge. *U.S. Army Photograph.*

Aerial cover in the Ardennes. *Photograph by Robert Capa/Magnum Photos, Inc.*

A German taken in the Bulge, probably around Bigonville,
December 1944. *Magnum Photos, Inc.*

The tragedy of Chaumont: A helmet, a jeep, and a corpse symbolize the
heaviness of the American loss, December 27, 1944.
*U.S. Army Photograph.*

After reserving MacAuliffe, 4th Armored soldiers guard German prisoners, December 27, 1944. *U.S. Army Photograph.*

Scene from the German counterattack in the Bulge, January 1945.
*U.S. Army Photograph.*

A dead German, a dead panzer: the Palatinate, March 1945.

General George S. Patton pisses into the Rhine River, March 24, 1945.

Sergeant Robert Saville.

Action on the Rhine, March 1945. *Photograph by Robert Capa/Magnum Photos, Inc.*

Nat's tank.

Gate of hell—Ohrdruf concentration camp, April 1943.

Patton, Ike, and Bradley view the victims of Nazi butchery, Ohrdruf,
April 1943. *U.S. Army Photograph.*

Ohrdruf—the best of the camps! *U.S. Army Photograph.*

Sergeant Nat Frankel.

General John Wood—the best
at his best, 1944.
*U.S. Army Photograph.*

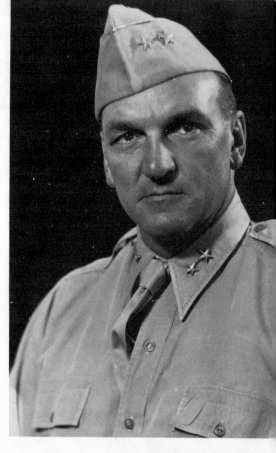

# 4

# Rivers of Darkness

"The die is cast," said Caesar after he crossed the Rubicon. In all war rivers are important, and they comprise a separate chapter in any history. The Rhine was of obvious significance to us, for the enemy's own ramparts were just on the other side. The Meuse and the Moselle were less vital, and crossing them would cast no dice, especially since the Battle of the Bulge was yet ahead. But they were there in any case, and sooner or later they had to be crossed.

The deepest meaning of a river is not simply that it is often a stupendous impediment to progress, thus necessitating a major tactical effort. In fact, the Meuse and the Moselle were both pretty accessible. They were shallow in many parts, and while our engineers may have had to build pontoons for other units attempting to cross in other parts, the 4th Armored, for one, simply drove across them. Similarly, our infantry detachments waded across, most often no more submerged in water than to their lower thighs. If I had to draw a comparison, I would refer you to the small rivers you see off the highway as you drive out for a Sunday picnic. They were considerably wider than these anonymous American streams—the Meuse and the Moselle are not, after all, rivulets—but they were no more forbidding in aspect.

No, the deepest military meaning of a river is not that it is physically difficult to cross. It is, rather, that they are automatic targets for defense. They're like signposts to the strategist. They mark off the terrain and form natural units of resistance. Don't let Patton cross the Meuse! If he does, stop him at the Moselle! Rivers are like integers on a number line. You can shuttle back and forth between 3 and 4, but just try to cross 4 and catch 5 in your binoculars and all hell might break loose.

It's also difficult to feel secure when you haven't got solid ground beneath your feet. Not that muddy, flaming earth, littered with corpses, makes for much security! But at least you've got something solid under you. Believe me, an infantryman hates being shot at while muddy water is swaying and splashing up to his crotch. Water is so goddamn amorphous, so unstable. I might go so far as to suggest that it's like being a baby again, or a fetus somewhere between birth and the darkness that precedes conception. That might be a pleasant enough sensation in the Bahamas, but it's excruciatingly unsettling when German soldiers are flinging shrapnel at your face. You want to grow up fast. And you can only grow up by getting out of the water and dying like a man on the solid earth of the far shore.

So as far as depth and width were concerned, the Meuse and the Moselle were accessible—but, in every other particular, they were as accessible as a bazooka in your worst enemy's hand. God knows, it took us long enough to cross both: ten days for the Meuse and twice that for the Moselle.

The Germans shelled all hell out of us at the Meuse. I have even heard reports that in some segments of the Third Army there was a rumor that the last German stand had been at the Meuse, that the route from the Moselle to Berlin would be gravy. Ha! I can guarantee that no one in the 4th Armored was dumb enough to believe that bullshit! But I will say that the Germans defended the Meuse like it was Hitler's own swimming pool, and the Moselle like it was his bathtub!

I have one weird and distinct memory of crossing the Meuse. The river was loaded with American tanks. To the Germans we must have looked like primeval beasts rising out of the turbid waters. But what I saw was stranger. There was a period of about ten minutes during which fiteen or twenty German shells must have exploded around us. I did not see one tank get hit. Yet the shells bursting in the water seemed to be falling symmetrically. As each one would hit, a narrow funnel of water would shoot up just behind. There was an odd geometry to these sudden and deadly fountains. They formed regular triangles, each point falling fifty yards ahead of me. There was nothing much to do but keep pushing forward, and as I did so, these lethal and yet ineffective triangles kept repeating their rigid formations just ahead of me. Death was splashing around me, but I couldn't help being mesmerized by these geometrics. It was almost pleasant.

That kind of hypnosis in war is commonplace, for horror brings with it a necessary disassociation. What was not commonplace was the actual fact that the German shells kept falling in these patterns. Once we were on the other side of the river, I asked three or four men from other tanks if they had seen the same symmetries and if they had been similarly mesmerized. They thought I was going bughouse, but thirty years later I'll still swear to the phenomenon.

Not that the other side of the Meuse gave us a world of time for chitchat! The German line was elastic, and had fallen back just far enough to secure a decent vantage point from which to pummel us. So we struggled all that day, ducking and sweating and bleeding for—for what? For an opportunity to cross another river, for a chance to wade across another shell-shocking flood of darkness!

That night we were able to sleep without much disturbance. Usually there would be interruptions from the sky. Though the Americans retained air superiority throughout the European war, there were, to be sure, some German intrusions. Bed Jack Charlie was the dog soldier's name for the enemy air presence.

It is striking that in the Vietnam War Charlie was the common name for the Vietcong.

At any rate, the skies above the east bank of the Meuse were reasonably quiet for a number of nights. One morning, however, about six A.M., just as we were beginning to push off for the day, an enormous noise of engines crackled in the still air. We looked up at a wobbly German transport plane flying too low for its own good and, considering the tactical changes of the preceding week, taking what was a precarious route. Our gunners shot it down, figuring they would deprive the enemy of some fuel or ammunition. But what we actually succeeded in depriving them of was neither fuel nor ammunition but something a little more harmless. And I might add that it was only a temporary deprivation at that.

I accompanied a small party to the site of the fallen plane. Two dead men, obviously the pilots, had been thrown some twenty-five yards in front of their machine. Their bodies were mangled and bleeding in every direction. But if those two men could have regained consciousness for a moment to give a howling utterance to the extent of their pain, it would not have been half so bloodcurdling as the scream that arose from the far side of the smoldering plane.

Twenty living, breathing females were running around in circles, beseeching the heavens for salvation, cursing existence for their fate, screaming at one another for God knows what reason. It was the oddest damn mixture of anger, terror, and just pure bitchiness! And what did we notice but that every single one of them had a Red Cross band on her arm. We weren't fooled at all. They were nurses like my mother was a weight lifter. Most of us figured that they were officers' wives.

About four or five of them were bleeding where they sat. Naturally these were the noisiest and angriest of all. If they were going to get raped or murdered, at least let them not suffer the indignity of a damaged backside! How cruel is life!

I know I sound callous, but I really can't stand officers' wives. They're basically an untrustworthy, self-seeking, and snooty lot. It is not, believe me, a productive role for a woman to fill. American wives are no exception. Occasionally you meet one with intelligence and charm who has gotten herself trapped in a world to which she herself is considerably superior. By and large, however, they comport themselves very poorly. In this situation the very shrillness of their behavior, their complete inability to face a situation they felt should only happen to a peasant, confirmed for us that they were indeed officers' wives.

But the best was yet to come. One of them spoke some English!

A lieutenant from my company had asked, or rather, had screamed above the din, if any of them spoke English. A thin blond, rubbing a nasty bruise on her upper arm, stepped forward. She took a deep breath, composed herself, conquered her terror, and spoke.

"Vee are nurses for our voonded."

"I'm sure," said the lieutenant, smiling as tenderly as he could and no doubt hoping against hope that the smile would not turn to laughter. I know I had the palm of my hand against my mouth in a similarly desperate attempt to keep my face straight.

"And zome of us are voonded."

"I can see that," said the lieutenant slyly.

That did it for some of us. A peal of laughter began to circulate among the Americans; the laughter must have frightened the "nurses" ' spokesperson, for she then said a wholly remarkable thing.

"Please not to do it to us."

That finished off the rest of us, myself included. I hadn't laughed like that since the last time I had gotten drunk. Now that lieutenant was doing yeoman's service; he should have gotten a medal. He reassured the "nurses" that they would be treated with all due propriety and would be returned as quickly as possible to their homes, vis-à-vis our headquarters. Which was indeed standard procedure for American forces. We never kept women prisoners; we apparently had a deal with the enemy to facilitate the return of women and children.

But the laughter was about to stop. We were sitting for something like two weeks waiting for the counterattack that would reportedly originate from the Moselle and attempt to push us back to the edge of the Meuse. Toward the end of this hiatus there occurred an incident that could have ruined my life and made incineration and death easily seem preferable to survival.

I was sitting in my turret, my hand resting on a .30-caliber machine gun. I knew that a counterattack could happen any-time. Company C was in an open field, some one hundred and fifty yards away from an elevated railroad track. Then I heard the sound of an army, of marching feet, the foreboding over-ture to combat.

Of the sixteen tanks in the company, mine was the closest to the bridge. If anyone were to open up, it would be me. The others would follow. I can't say that I froze; no, I wasn't afraid at all, certainly not at this point. But something made me hold back. To this day I can't define what it was. Perhaps it was just an inkling, an instinctive warning inside that made me wait until I could see the whites of their eyes. Well, maybe not. I had a .50-caliber machine gun behind me, but even if I had opened up with the .30-caliber, I would have done great damage without even seeing at whom I was firing. Then the other tanks could have joined me, and together we would have dealt a crushing first-round jab to this "counterattack."

So what kept me from firing? I just don't know. It would even be too easy to attribute my pause to divine interces-sion. No, it was just something wholly gratuitous, the kind of inscrutable luck whose source we can never locate and whose purpose we can only guess at.

I waited, fingered the trigger, waited another two or three seconds. And then I saw the troops. You've probably guessed by now. They were Americans. Had I opened up ten seconds earlier, I would have killed at least one-hundred of my own comrades. Their lives weren't worth any more than the German lives I took, but in war you have to keep your sanity by drawing the line somewhere. You have to draw a line that superimposes rhyme and reason on all the killing. To cross that line is to lose your mind.

So what had happened? Information concerning the coming passage of an American company over this bridge had come in while I was asleep. Every other tank in the company knew it, which is probably why they didn't open up or shout to me to do so. Even the other guys in my tank knew what was really going on. The man—and this man will remain forever nameless—whom I had relieved had awakened me from a deep sleep. "Your turn, Sarge," he had said. But he himself was so sleepy that it never occurred to him that I ought to know about this troop movement.

I couldn't even scream at him later. "What can I say? I'm sorry," he said. My face must have registered all the admonition necessary. And my brush with disaster, with catastrophic guilt, had been so precarious, the consequences for my own peace of mind would have been so monumental, that any scolding on my part would have been fatuous.

I don't think the Germans we encountered at the Moselle expected to survive the war. Since they had nothing to lose, they fought with awesome, reckless ferocity. And they were well trained, too. The far side of the river was loaded with Tiger 6 tanks: big, powerful mothers! The shelling itself was only half our problem: The sight of those masterful Germans on the other side was considerably more forbidding. In fact, I have no memory of any tank getting hit by shells during the actual crossing of either the Meuse or the Moselle. The infantry no doubt caught a lot more hell.

But you'd better believe we lost machinery and men as we came out of the river. The tank next to mine lost its whole treading from the fire of a German tank gun, and men were falling on the far banks like bowling pins. Whenever men die in front of water, it always looks the same. It looks like abortion, like the life of a man or the conception of an attack suddenly cut down just as it emerges from the primal, liquid womb. That was the way Omaha and Utah beaches looked, and that was the way the Moselle looked. Only the scale was smaller, but the Germans wanted that goddamn river.

I would later learn that there had been fierce competition between the First and Third Armies to cross the Moselle and breach the West Wall beyond. The West Wall was the German defense line that extended from Cleves to the Swiss border. I cannot emphasize too strongly that this sort of competitiveness was strictly a higher-echelon preoccupation. The soldiers themselves weren't aware of this "race" and couldn't care less. We were grown men, for Chrissakes, which is a lot more than can be said for many officers.

Just to set the record straight, however—and my subsequent readings tell me that the record needs straightening—the 4th Armored Division was the first American unit to cross the Moselle—on September 11, 1944. It was the First Army who won the race to breach the West Wall.

It was Lt. William Marshall whose tank first crossed the Moselle, and thus he merits a particular place in the history of the 4th Armored. For being first Marshall was awarded the Distinguished Service Cross. He would later return to his native Newark and become a cop. In recognition of his war service the city never made him take a civil service test.

I can guarantee that no one in the 4th Armored was the least bit impressed by his having been the first to cross the river. We knew too much. We knew that he just happened to have been in the right place at the right time. Eventually, he got himself captured during the run to Bastogne.

The whole Moselle campaign was not one of Patton's brightest moments. He must be taken to task for underestimating German strength and for pressing the river too thinly. A greater concentration of strength at any given point would have forced a more effective, certainly a quicker, beachhead. It is true that Patton's superiors were diverting supplies and troops from Lorraine and the rivers, but even Patton's idolators admit his tactical miscalculations at this juncture.

But the Moselle was eventually secured, and we awaited the First Army, whose units would breach the West Wall. The fighting on the far side of the river was fierce, but I must admit that I cherish its memory. One of those incidents occurred that humanizes war as much as possible, that injects a humor, however grim, into the otherwise purely brutal proceedings.

A monster of a Tiger 6 was pivoting not thirty yards in front of me. I fired three shots at it, figuring to force it backward. All three shots bounced off the side and ricocheted harmlessly. What do I see but a German officer stick his head out of the turret and smile at me! He then proceeded to pull a white handkerchief out of his pocket and wipe it against the side of his machine, where my bullets had skidded. He smiled again as if to forgive me for scratching his property; then he replaced his handkerchief in his pocket. I would give my right arm to know that officer's name and his present whereabouts.

And now we were deep in the heart of Lorraine. The Germans were not about to withdraw without a counterattack; what had been rumor after the Meuse was now an inevitability. The German objective was Nancy, which they could gain by outflanking us at Lunéville. In this attempt the finest of panzer divisions were engaged. We lost at least two hundred and fifty men before we mopped them up; Nancy was permanently ours. As always, General Wood was up front and frequently accessible. In fact, his presence during this whole push into Lorraine is, in retrospect, particularly memorable, since this was his last campaign with the 4th Armored.

The landscape was muddy; a few barren trees dotted the earth. It was getting cold. In a sense, Lunéville was our first taste of what our drive to close the Belfort Gap just before the Bulge would be like. Here, however, the terrain seemed to bother the Germans more. As great as these panzers were, our speed and the inclement conditions befuddled them. Only a massive German artillery barrage extended the battle to the week or so that it lasted.

But what artillery! We had no choice but to push forward, for our whole rear was smoking. (Indeed, a frequent tactical drawback of artillery overkill is that it sometimes forces the enemy to a continuous, desperate advance. And sometimes those advances gain the day.) I saw an enormous explosion from an .88 shell take out a tank just in front of me. Its commander was a good friend, a fellow named Horvath from Ohio, who was killed. His gunner, a kid named Michaelovich from Binghamton, New York, was cut completely in half. His upper torso was at his feet. He looked like a broken mannequin. A bullet in the forehead is one thing, but you'd think a man has a right to some dignity in death. What is it that makes a grizzly death grizzly? It is not the blood and guts, the untimeliness, the pain. It is, rather, the complete loss of human dignity, of even looking human. That's what grizzly means.

And then the town of Lunéville was so quiet, so quaint: rows of two-story houses, with sleepy eaves dripping gracefully over the tops. Our next stop would be Arracourt, supposedly a rest stop—but there would be another counterattack, and we'd have to fight like hell just for the pleasure of a shave and shower in an uncontested village. And all the while other units of the Third Army were battering Metz to the north, a three-month siege destined to end only in late November. Before Singling, before the Battle of the Bulge, we'd be joining that siege.

# 5
# Attila's Town

The Third Army hurled itself against Metz for three months, beginning its siege sometime in early September. Patton was not within its walls until November 25, 1944, and the 4th Armored was not involved with the entire effort. We were brought up from our Moselle beachhead in early November, and some of us remained there until the end. My own company did not; we returned to Arracourt in time for the Belfort push. It was really my only taste of failure in the war: firing and bombarding, throwing flame and death and seeing yourself fired upon and dying—all to no avail. That the Americans did eventually take the town does not change my point. When I left the Metz area, it was with the bitterest taste in my mouth.

When I think of Metz, a kind of daydream of war formulates itself in my mind. It is a daydream I remember taking shape soon after we left Metz, one that has stayed with me ever since. It is a fantasy of another war—World War I—and it is appropriate that it should be anachronistic, for Metz itself was of another time, another world.

I see a soldier flat on his stomach, crawling forward over muddy, cold no-man's-land. It is the western front in 1917 or 1918. His company has been ordered to take an enemy position some thousand yards away, across the inflamed and polluted plain. The enemy resistance is tumultuous. Shells are exploding everywhere, and the soldier cannot even see his own men crawling with him. Every few minutes he has to bury his face in the mud to avoid the inevitable shrapnel. When he picks his face up out of the muck, his lips are coated with thick water, his eyes nearly blinded with filth. If he finds a second or two for thought, if any fragment of his life flashes before him, it is the memory or consciousness of some past failure. Or it is the recollection of a circumstance or relationship that he now sees as a failure for the first time. The mud and the din are transforming everything, past and future, into the wretched substance of mud and din.

Suddenly the shelling stops. The soldier doesn't know why, but he instinctively assumes that the enemy is regrouping for a final, major bombardment. And so he crawls even more determinedly, never looking to his back or to his side. Ahead of him he sees a ridge and just behind it the enemy. He figures he'll be hurling himself over it with his comrades in one savage charge. The enemy will fall back, intimidated, their shells now useless to them.

He attains the ridge, almost like a suicide attains the pavement after a jump from a skyscraper. He leaps over, yawping fiercely. His gun waves at his side. Four or five enemy soldiers whirl about in surprise as they see him. But there is no shooting. Instead, the enemy laughs hilariously, almost mockingly. The soldier lands on his feet and covers them with his gun, staring blindly at these laughing adversaries whom he has "captured." One of them walks toward him, places his hand on his shoulder, and leads him to the hem of the ridge. He points back over the plain from which the soldier has come. What the soldier sees amazes him. There on the plain is his entire company: dead! Only he has made the ridge. He is the advance guard. His defeat is total, but he joins the enemy in laughter, for the values of steadfastness and courage and unyielding perseverance have suddenly lost their meaning for him.

This daydream continued to haunt me after Metz, even though I did not crawl through any mud, nor did I lose my whole company. But I was taught the meaning of defeat there as we pulled away from the still untaken city, to return to Arracourt and rest. Yet even before Metz we would have to fight and many of us to die for that resting place. I would well remember that fight for Arracourt, for I lost one of my best friends there.

Early in this memoir I mentioned that of the five of us who were intimately friendly and who expected to die—myself, Andy Cammerary, Bob Saville, Paul Glaz, and George Cardge —only one of us did indeed perish. This was George Cardge. During the battle for Arracourt some shrapnel got him. He was in the turret at the wrong time. I saw him grasp his head with his hands. Then his knees wobbled and he swayed slowly down. When I reached his body, I turned him over and saw two hollow, unblinking eyes gaping up at me.

Upset as I was about George's death, I wasn't surprised. There was something miserably inevitable about it, as if George had been the most likely candidate of my friends to go. He never seemed as tough or as flamboyant as Andy or Paul or Bob. There was something vulnerable about him, something tender. Just before the preceding fight at Lunéville, George had received word that his wife was pregnant.

The fight for Arracourt was generally upsetting. History records that we mopped up the Germans, and that's true. We were still dealing with ace panzers, and we creamed them. But history makes Arracourt seem like a very routine victory, like an easy foul shot when you're fifteen points ahead to begin with. That's not the case. In reality, I remember a kind of all-pervasive despair as we fought for that village, right on the heels of a similar struggle for Lunéville. We didn't seem to be going anywhere. True, we were always winning, but so what?

We were still sticking to the Moselle area like glue, and who knew but that the Germans might send counteroffensives against us there forever? In such a situation, winning is as futile as losing. So in a way, the move to Metz was a kind of relief, even though our efforts there were delayed and embittered. But Arracourt came first, and if we fought with particular savagery, it was probably because we felt stifled—as if we were tearing away membranous prisons around us, only to find another tissue afterward. And then to lose George! . . .

I remember a German infantryman dying at Arracourt. He lay a few hundred yards away from my tank. From my vantage point, it seemed he had a vicious stomach wound. He kept raising his arms above him, suspending them in the air for a moment. Then they'd wave around a second or two, weakly and randomly, and then drop. He seemed to be trying to beseech the heavens for salvation, but he lacked the strength to keep his arms in a beseeching position. The cliché is that there are no atheists in a foxhole, but not being an atheist didn't do this poor son of a bitch any good. I took a shot at him, figuring to end his misery. But I missed.

That soldier, and all the ones like him, would be cleared away by the time we backed off from Metz to rest at Arracourt. The smoke would be cleared, the air crisp and quiet. And we all enjoyed that town, myself included. There would be moments when George's ghost would hover around, but for the sake of my own sanity I brushed him aside. But I wish I didn't have to. I wish he could have died somewhere else where I didn't have to spend so much time.

Now, frustration was not the only dimension of the Metz experience. Indeed, that experience was one of the more picturesque aspects of the European war. For Patton Metz was a historic challenge, a real touchstone for his own notion of himself as a mythical warrior. In fact, the Third Army was originally going to ignore the whole city. It was not strategically imperative. But what a plum it seemed to Patton! It had been taken by Attila the Hun in the middle of the fifth century and was a bone of contention between the French and the Germans throughout the early periods of modern history.

In addition, Metz was probably the most heavily fortified city in Europe. They were not Nazi fortifications: not those medieval ramparts and conical forts! The Germans would have needed quite a sense of humor to have built such a city. No, these were from the Middle Ages, and they had defied the tactical acumen of countless generals over the centuries. Now it was Patton's turn to storm the thirty-seven forts that ringed Metz. What made it even tougher was that these forts were all interconnected by a series of tunnels. This meant two things: First, any particular fort could be quickly reinforced by supplies or men from another. Second, the structure of the tunnels leading to the center of the city began on the outskirts. Thus, the Germans were able to position their artillery well away from the direct access points and establish a brutally tough buffer against attack. When I was there with the 4th Armored, we were never any closer than ten miles without.

And yet my mind had been prepared for the bizarre sight of a medieval city successfully resisting a modern technological onslaught. This preparation came during the journey from Arracourt to Metz, which included a phenomenon as weirdly anachronistic as any wooden drawbridge. It was a phenomenon that, I might add, we would see more of in Germany proper, but the road to Metz was my first taste of it.

I am speaking of the little monolithic "pillboxes" the Germans spread across the countryside. Often there would not be enough time for planting a mine; moreover, it was impossible to lay enough mines to halt the progress of an entire battalion, let alone division. So they would take these three- to four-foot concrete slabs, implant them in hardened soil, and cover the entire diameter of a field or plain.

They looked like little stone idols, miniature Stonehenges erected to the gods, fetishes against the ancestral and relentless enemy. And that enemy was us. Often a whole afternoon would be wasted blowing out or digging up these impediments. I can tell you, it was a weird experience to be driving along and suddenly see a deep row of flat monoliths glistening in the sun; it was like coming upon a ring of skulls in the jungle, which state with terrifying definiteness that the territory beyond is taboo. The medieval circumference of Metz merely climaxed this strange time warp, this odd backsliding to the military modes of ancient worlds.

Patton's plans for Metz had bogged down in agony by the time we reached the city. His main thrust had been against Fort Driant, but it wasn't giving and wouldn't give until well after our withdrawal back to Arracourt. We stood outside the city for days, simply blowing our guns against the walls, and ducking as best we could the fierce German artillery barrages. I saw three tanks hit within two days. I can remember the sinking feeling, the desperate men scrambling out of the burning tanks, the total immobility—and I wondered how those sturdy and proud towers could ever be made to crumble.

But the weirdest sight of all was the specter of some of the towers actually crumbling. It was as if we were blowing the Middle Ages away with our shells and guns so far beyond the dreams of any baron or king or pope. At the highest points of Metz were conical rooftops sitting heavily atop fat cylindrical supports. It was like the set for some cinematic pageantry, a stubborn affront to all the changes that history and technology had wrought. And then to fill your gun, your twentieth-century gun, and fire it and watch the ancient ramparts fall—why, it was like the pouring of the seven vials, and we were the bloody angels unraveling the textures of apocalypse. But on whose behalf? On God's? Of course not. God had always been most welcome in the Middle Ages; the old planks of Metz had seen His presence a thousand times or more. We were blowing away the shape of an inveterate, noble world on behalf of a modern, godless world, which even Patton himself hated and feared. But it was the Nazis who had wormed their way inside the old fortress, and so it had to go.

I regret not being there with Patton when Metz was finally taken. How haunting a sight it must have been, a real picture of the castle keep taken by the fierce and unpredictable intruder from the barren tundras of the North or the swarthy plateaus of the South. Despite the sense of frustration I brought away with me when I did leave, I'm glad I saw Metz, if only for the vision of those heavy-grained turrets falling to our twentieth-century insistence. After all, not every man lives to see centuries of history encapsulated in one battle!

The road back to Arracourt was clear—we were the ones who had cleared it—and we made it back without significant incident. And yet even this mild journey backward was haunting and, in a way, played on us the same kind of tricks with time as the pillboxes and the ramparts of Metz had played. I think all the men of the 4th Armored experienced a provocative déjà vu. We came abreast Nancy—that's where we had rested just before the counterattack at Arracourt. And the landscape itself—so peaceful, like a camping trip in the Adirondacks, but the soil, we realized, had been drenched and fertilized with nearly fresh blood, our blood. And then Arracourt itself, where I lay my head on a bundle of straw—for which I could thank Gen. Holmes Dager. Dager? Just as the counteroffensive at Arracourt had begun, Dager had called John Wood.

"John, you need some straw for your boys? You must be tired. I can send some over."

"Straw, my ass! I got a war here!"

The Dagers never know. The Woods always do. *Requiescat in pace.*

While describing the shape of Metz, I recalled a novel by William Eastlake called *Castle Keep*, in which a detachment of American soldiers finds sanctuary inside a late medieval manor. Eastlake's fiction reminds me in turn of the problems encountered by any man who would recount the actual feeling of war.

It may be that the actual reality of war is so overwhelming that it is almost impossible to take stock of it. And that stock-taking process is in itself crippling to any further effort. I've seen veterans just bubbling over with memory, with an actual lust to tell their tales of Armageddon. But once they start, even the most articulate of them fall tongue-tied. What was Iwo Jima like? It was . . . it was . . . it was fucking rough, man! I know that, but what was it like? Really . . . really . . . really tough! So the very experience of war, what would seem to be the prerequisite for describing it, precludes any actual, palpable narrative.

Only once, in Erich Remarque's *All Quiet on the Western Front*, have I ever been made to feel that the author was sitting in the one and only stadium where this unique and horrific game was being played.

Or maybe twice. The other book I'm thinking of really punctuates my point, for it is the exception that proves the rule. Stephen Crane wrote *The Red Badge of Courage* without ever actually having been in the Civil War. Had he been, would these monumental experiences of life and death have twisted his tongue? I think so. Crane would have started the novel and given it up; or he would have finished it, but it would not have survived.

I'd like to bring up another subject vital to any total assessment of a military campaign: the subject of love and sex. I cannot imagine any lovers anywhere talking to each other like they do in *A Farewell to Arms* and *For Whom the Bell Tolls*. And in the middle of a war, ridiculous! First of all, no son of a bitch lying in an army hospital ever had sex with a nurse! It's such a cheap fantasy, such soap opera shit! And that in turn damages the credibility of Hemingway's combat scenes—for what can we believe after he's treated us to such an obvious lie?

Actually, however, I do know of a soldier who had sex with a nurse, but this one instance is so ludicrous, so much a parody of normal human relations, that it puts Hemingway to even greater shame. A friend of mine I met after the war was in a hospital in Oran. In the bed next to him was a soldier with a minor groin wound, but serious enough to have warranted some elaborate stitching. Every day this same nurse would spend more than her normal tour time by his bed. Who knows, maybe they had been lovers beforehand.

One night my friend was lying awake contemplating the dingy ceiling. He heard someone tip-toe in, realized it was the nurse, and so closed his eyes. She went to her friend's bed and there initiated a sexual act that required no movement on the soldier's part. My friend smiled to himself and began to fall asleep. Suddenly the night was rent by a piercing shriek. My friend sat up in alarm and saw the soldier rolling over off the bed in hideous pain. Now how shall we phrase this with all due delicacy? Suffice it to say that the normal physiological response of a male to sexual stimulation had succeeded in ripping his stitches. A farewell to *arms*? Maybe!

What, then, is the reality of love and sex amid the conflagration of an entire continent? The average soldier who landed at Utah Beach and survived to take Germany, the man who was neither stud nor sissy, probably slept with something like twenty-five women during the war—and few of them were, I might add, prostitutes. But the sexuality of the dogface in Europe was neither flamboyant nor sentimental, nor was it callous. There was great desperation in it and considerable satisfaction, but, just as it often began with terrible yearning, it often finished that way, too: with yearning of a deep and multifaceted character.

One must remember the situation of the participants. Most of the women we had were—contrary to the popular portrait of hungry, hot French girls running away from their shopkeeper fathers—Germans, women who in many cases hadn't seen their husbands or lovers in five years. In some instances, this made for another problem. Being with the woman was sheer anonymity. The soldier knew that he was merely a substitute. He knew that he could have been just anyone.

And his attitudes were agonizingly complex for still other reasons. The typical soldier gives himself up for dead before he ever sees combat. And then the combat experience itself merely reinforces this sense of doom. So every woman might be his last. This is a cliché, but a truthful and powerful one— particularly if you can imagine what it's like to make love while assuming that tomorrow you'll be dead. You are no more violent in bed than usual. In fact, you're not even necessarily more loving. But perhaps you clutch the girl's shoulders a little more firmly than you normally would.

The girl, meanwhile, even as she's dreaming of her real lover, knows what you're thinking. She herself is torn; while pretending you're someone else, she's simultaneously relating to the actual and awful fact that she's in bed with a man who knows he may die. So watch her face; she alternately opens and closes her eyes, sometimes in ecstacy, more often in a desperate attempt to grasp this essentially ungraspable situation. And she stares up at you with the slightest hint of guilt in her eyes—or is that knitted brow simply the knowledge, flowing into her mind like you into her body, of what she herself must mean to you, a man whose name she'll not remember? Watch her face because she's watching yours.

She's very accommodating, too. She'll do anything for you— for you as her distant lover, and for the real you as well, the stranger who may die tomorrow. If you're a decent fellow, you demand a lot of love and you get it. If you're a pig, the girl is unlucky but can't say no anyway. I knew some soldiers who procured some pretty bizarre favors from women. In a situation like this the woman doesn't even feel decent saying no to the Marquis de Sade.

But whatever she does, it's not enough for you. It can't be. Women are only human, after all, and war is something more.

So you stare down at this German soldier's wife, and, for all you've gone through and will go through, she seems unreal. Unreal, like a whore seems unreal. But she's not a whore. And you've got to remember that she's not a whore. If her husband survives, he'll come back to pick up their lives again. He'll silently assume she's slept with someone, probably an American, but if he's any kind of a man, he'll never ask.

She might already be a widow. Perhaps even a virgin—for who knows, what with Hitler's dream crashing down so monstrously, if without you she would ever have lived to be anything but a virgin? So she takes it now, while she can. I remember another woman, who was neither widow nor virgin, who had slept with a soldier in my company. Once I saw her outside with this man, just before we were ready to resume our lightning dash through Germany. She began to tug at his uniform, but the man was embarrassed; he walked away, slowly, his head slightly bent. Then she looked at me, not asking me to come to her but just looking—at me and through me. Just looking. Not even waiting. Just looking.

Later on many of them became whores. Present-day Europe is full of respectable, petty-bourgeois women who have, at least once in their lives, flung back their legs for the price of a loaf of bread. But who's to judge? Many of them I saw were completely incapable of playing the role of whore with any conviction. I remember one whore in particular. We were deep in Germany, and I asked her if her husband was still alive. Like the woman who had grabbed at the soldier's clothes, she just looked at me. She wasn't waiting. She was just looking, just looking. Sex can be jagged glass.

Maybe I was right before. Maybe our twentieth-century guns did blow away the Middle Ages when we bombarded the nearly impregnable castles of Metz. But some things you can't blow away. Some things never change.

# 6
# Closing the
# Belfort Gap

We rested at Arracourt and then embarked on one of the epic struggles of World War II. Now, I'm not talking about the Bulge, or Stalingrad, or the Battle of Britain, or Guadalcanal. I'm talking about something that only the soldiers themselves, plus only a handful of historians, remember. Even the historians who do remember it give it short shrift in their records of the Third Army. I'm talking about the brief campaign to close the Belfort Gap and the excruciating effort to get there.

"Epic struggle" is not a bullshit hyperbole. I suppose that, for the historian or writer, war is an embarrassment of riches. You've got all these cannons going off everywhere, literally all over the world. Even the most assiduous scholarship is likely to neglect one. But when we talk about the Belfort Gap, we're not just discussing tens of thousands of lives tossed around like shit in a trough. We're discussing a whole machine of men throwing itself against the earth for a month, a whole machine of men clawing and biting at unyielding ground, grabbing at it with their hands and guns and knives and tanks. Fighting for every inch of ground—that's not hyperbole either. I'm telling you that for every bit of forward movement, a human being was extinguished.

In fact, I remember a very strange thought, a kind of mental paralysis, that came to me. I was standing outside my tank about halfway to Belfort and began to nonchalantly walk forward. I came even with the front of my machine, and then suddenly halted. For an instant I was afraid to push myself any further, not even a half inch further, than my tank had carried me. The concept of the ground itself had for that instant become so heightened that I imagined that to presume to walk an extra inch would unleash some new shell-shocking fury. But I got over it. You get over everything eventually, one way or another.

So I call it an epic struggle, but I don't think Homer or Virgil could have understood it.

The men of the 4th Armored called it the Battle of Singling. But Singling was only one of a million towns we took during this winter drive; it was ten miles from the German border, and it happened to be a particularly rugged objective. It was, however, a name meaningful only to the 4th Armored; the campaign of which it formed a part was much larger than any one town. The Seventh Army was involved as well as the Third; as such, the strategy, which was to reach the Saar and seize Alsace-Lorraine,was mainly Ike's—certainly not Patton's.

The Seventh was commanded by Gen. Alexander Patch, a good soldier and an old friend of Patton's. The idea was to bring the Seventh way up from the south, while we were to meet them at the enemy-held Belfort Gap. Though we had just bridged the Moselle, Arracourt had been a good rest, and we were more or less ready—ready for what can be seen in retrospect as an important transitional phase between the Normandy–Brittany–northern France chapter of the war and the race to the Rhine and our long mad dash across Germany.

When we left Arracourt, we sailed slowly but smoothly for ten miles. Then hell. Now hell wasn't just Hitler and his frustrated generals. Hell was Mother Nature, too. The sky above looked like Gary, Indiana. Bleak, baby. The ground was an ice bed of mud. You could see leaves of grass frozen like mummies beneath thin coats of frost. And it was even worse where the ice wasn't predominant. Cakes of mud were rising up like lava. Each step was a major effort. At some points it seemed you needed a pulley to lift your foot out of that shit. When I think of what the infantry must have been going through, I could kiss my tank and every goddamn tank ever manufactured.

But the worst of it wasn't the ice or the mud or the sky; the worst was the snow. The snow wasn't so much of an impediment as it was a constant mirror of battle. You see, the snow was stained with blood, rivers of it. At one point, we saw whole patches of red dotting an otherwise white landscape. Poets may talk about snow as if it were some sort of symbol of purity, but that's all shit to me. Red on white, red on white—it looked as if a bride had been butchered in her wedding bed.

We had damn good infantry with us, too; we damn well had to have good infantry with us. I would single out the 26th as a courageous, uncomplaining host of heroes. But then we had detachments from the 14th Armored as well. There was nothing wrong with them except that they were raw. The 4th had to take the initiative. In fact, as we'll soon see, if the march to Belfort had one unique characteristic, it was the mounting presence of inexperienced combatants, in some cases men who were not even supposed to be firing guns. But I'll get back to that.

By the time we had blown and crawled halfway to Belfort, it was impossible to evacuate our wounded by ambulance. The mud and ice were simply too much. The last ambulance at Singling that I can remember seeing glided on the ice and turned over, spilling its wounded like a grave spitting up corpses at the Last Judgment. After that they used light tanks to rescue the fallen. The men were put on stretchers, passed hand over hand to the top of the tanks, and then driven to the field hospitals. It was an eerie sight, a daily grotesquerie: wounded, bleeding men being fed to their metallic saviors.

I remember one man, a curly-haired infantryman with a vicious hole in his chest, who completely lost touch with reality. He saw himself being lifted to the tank and got it into his skull that we were sending him back into combat. I suppose there was a method to his madness. He was half out of it, and all he knew was that he was being put in a tank. "I'm too sick to kill," he screamed. Then the medic told him that he was going to the field hospital. But the kid just screamed back, "I want to go to the hospital." And the medic screamed back that that's exactly where he was going. But once again the soldier demanded to be taken to the hospital. It went on like that with the two screaming madly at each other—take me to the hospital that's where you're going take me to the hospital that's where you're going—like some married couples I know, until the tank finally left.

I spent a little while—two days, in fact—in the hospital, but I didn't have to be lifted onto any light tank. There's a condition, first reported in World War I, known as trench foot. It wasn't until long after Normandy that the medics figured it out and were able to stop it. It's nothing more, really, than a loss of circulation in the foot due to tight shoes and unrelieved pressure. But for a while nobody knew what to do about it, and many were the men who developed gangrene and lost their legs altogether. Wars have been lost because of small things like trench foot. By the time of Singling, however, a quick trip to the doctor, who elevated and swathed the foot, was sufficient.

Anyway, one night I got down on my hands and knees and pleaded with God to give me trench foot. At the risk of understatement, I'll say that I needed a rest. That day had been one of continuous shelling, and I had seen one too many severed head and far too many frozen, dangling blood vessels. Son of a bitch if the next day I don't wake up with trench foot, unable to walk at all. There were no light tanks by us at the time, so, using a mechanic as support, I hobbled behind the line and reported sick. I sat two days with my leg up, while the man who replaced me in the turret took some shrapnel and has been completely paralyzed since. But those kinds of reprieves soon begin to run off your back like water.

Who knows, I may have induced trench foot myself by simply wanting it so awfully badly. But why analyze? I'll give God credit for this one.

So many men were wounded en route to the Belfort Gap and the movement was so slow that there were times we simply received no replacements at all. I fought through at least half of Singling with three men in the tank instead of five. I had lost one man not long after the fighting started outside Arracourt. This gentleman, who shall remain nameless, had taken a revolver, placed the muzzle around five inches from his leg, and pulled the trigger. I could have shot him for that, but I reported it as an accident, and he was out of the war. There are guys who can face off five apes in a bar but simply can't take combat. And then there are other men who are mice in civilian life, but in the context of war, in the well-structured and sanctioned atmosphere of mass murder, they can go hell-bent-for-leather. I think it's because they know there's no way out. And yet that same restriction, which enables meek men to fight bravely, entails for other, more pugnacious men, a claustrophobia that's simply intolerable.

So I didn't kill the "coward." I'm not George Patton, for Chrissakes. I'll do his bidding, I'll kill the Hun for him, but what law says I have to adopt his values and judge others accordingly? I prayed for two days' rest, and a man who stood in my place was paralyzed. Was I a coward? If so, a man's life was ruined as a result. If you think I should have been shot, to hell with you!

The other man I lost took some shrapnel in his skull while standing outside our tank. I can't really tell you much about him; he was a nondescript sort of fellow. Usually the nondescript ones survive longer than the personality kids, but this guy just fell over one afternoon as though his legs had suddenly turned to jelly.

Not only didn't we get the human reinforcements we needed, but supplies couldn't keep up with us either. So what do you do? You walk, baby, that's what you do. We'd bivouac at night, and then carry our gasoline and ammunition back to the line with us. Not one tank was allowed to double back, not one tank could leave its hard-won clod of stinking earth, to pick up supplies. And I didn't resent that, either, not when each one of those clods was so costly we wanted to wrap it up and send it home to mother.

But the walks were a special kind of hell, for reasons far more extraordinary than our simple craving for rest. The Germans, you see, were a cute collection of people. At night they would use a shell, a special kind of shell, which, in itself, did no more or no less damage than any other kind of shell. But this particular device was loud, loud, loud. They used it as psychological warfare, a premeditated attempt to drive the enemy out of its ever-loving mind. In thousands of cases they probably succeeded. We called them screaming meemies. Imagine, if you will, a police siren reverberating through a complex of cavernous hills and valleys, and each time its sound bounces off one hill, it amplifies its volume threefold. It wasn't just a screech from hell; it was all of hell concentrating itself, expressing itself, in one long wailing blast. And at night, after the bullets and the shells, after the frozen corpses and the blood-stained snow, you're walking, walking, walking, your back loaded with supplies and your ears with this ungodly sound. Quite a concept, the screaming meemie.

Sometimes—but mercifully not too often—the Germans would release the screaming meemies during the day. I remember sitting in my tank during a lull in the fighting. I gazed around and just happened to see a soldier standing by the road urinating. Then came a screaming meemie. But as I began to screw up my face in an effort to tolerate the din, I saw something that for that moment diverted my attention even from the sound itself. The soldier was still relieving himself as the shell flew over. The din rattled him completely, and he dropped his head back perpendicular to his neck and shrieked. The image of a human being pissing in one direction and howling in another is stamped permanently in my mind's eye.

I mentioned earlier that Singling was marked by the presence of many soldiers who were either raw or totally untrained for combat. This fact related to the inability of trained combatants to reach us at all. So instead they gave us everyone and anyone. Men from ordnance and Quartermaster, cooks, and mechanics became, about halfway to Belfort, fighting men. And, if you will recall, the air force was still a unit of the army at the time. So, sure enough, we had airmen in our tanks as well, and the infantry had pilots with them too, slogging by foot through the icy mires.

I'd like to spend a little time on these noncombatants, not only because their presence distinguished Singling but because it made for a different kind of war altogether. One day a man at Quartermaster is handing you blankets, trying like hell to be friendly, and maybe even feeling a little guilty that you'll be catching action while he'll be reading girlie magazines in the storeroom. Or if he isn't feeling guilty, he's uncomfortable because, like a hunter's wife, he doesn't know if you'll ever be requisitioning supplies again. In fact, there's something rather female about his role.

And then what? Then he's in your tank looking to you for salvation, his knees trembling, his lips quivering. He's looking to you to explain all this to him, and you haven't got the time.

Or an ordnance man. An expert on guns. A man who knows bullets. Canny, canny. Knows logistics. He knows all the details, the mechanics, the material of war. What he doesn't know is the form of war. War itself. I remember one guy they brought up who within the hour was just cursing to himself, muttering "oh shit! oh shit!" for what seemed like hours. I should have broken his jaw.

And so it's a different kind of war because suddenly there's a dearth of warriors. You—Sergeant Frankel—you're the warrior, and you feel awfully, desperately alone when you find you have to be leading men who don't belong there. To be the *only* warrior in the midst of apocalypse, that's a lonely concept. But it could have been much worse. I at least knew that I was with the 4th Armored Division and that every other seasoned figher beyond my immediate vision was worth a thousand legitimate replacements.

At times it was almost funny—well, perhaps *laughable* is a better term. There was a mechanic in my tank named Green, a likable fellow who wore these thick, horn-rimmed glasses. I had known him well enough to talk to him, since he was also from New York and we had at least a little in common. After his arrival as a "combatant," we were standing some seven feet away from each other.

"Hello, Mazursky," he said.

"Frankel," I corrected him, figuring he had forgotten my name.

He walked about three feet closer, craned his neck forward, and said, "Oh! Nat! I thought you were Mazursky."

All I could see was my own reflection in those opaque glasses of his. "Jesus goddamn Christ, Green! Are you blind?"

"Just don't let me fire at any of our own boys," he said.

I still don't know whether or not he was serious. Green survived, I think, but there were others who were more pathetic. I remember one man—he must have been thirty-five if he was a day—who wet his pants and then wept in shame. And all the while we had to teach these men how to fight. There were long hours in the turret when I was literally showing men how to feed bullets to the gun. Could they shoot straight? They couldn't even hold the gun right! In the midst of the toughest fighting of the Third Army's campaign (and, again, I don't mean to underestimate the race to Bastogne), I was teaching men what I had learned in basic training.

Yes, a different kind of war. There was one kid—and I mean

kid—from Quartermaster who was up in the turret with me. I was screaming instructions at him because the shelling was deafening. And he kept jumping, particularly when we heard the sound of our track pummeled with bullets. I felt like sitting on him. I shouted to him to load and fire himself. "What?" he screamed back. I repeated myself. Then he shouted something else at me. I couldn't hear him the first or second time, but the third time I knew what he was saying.

"I might get killed," he was saying. His exact words. About ten or fifteen sarcastic replies formulated themselves in my head, but I couldn't get any of them out. I just nodded, and I hoped to hell that the expression on my face was at least sympathetic.

During the lulls in combat, the regular noncombatants were, almost to a man, quiet, almost sullen. The only exceptions went in the opposite direction; they wouldn't stop chattering. The men of the 4th did their best to comfort them, but within a few days it just made more sense to avoid them.

I remember sitting with an infantry officer. It was during a lull some five miles away from the gap itself, where the final fierce climax was yet to occur.

"Wait and see," he said. "After the war, we'll be talking about how savage the Germans were for using unqualified men as cannon fodder. Nobody will ever remember that we sent our cooks out to fight."

What was also so odd was the contempt with which even the gentlest of us viewed these unqualified victims of tactical necessity. It was a contempt that was certainly mixed with pity, but I think there's always something disgusting about victims. You can't help it. I remember one phrase the men of the 4th used most often when referring to these cooks, blanket distributors, and shell counters. We called them poor sons of bitches, and we almost smiled when we said it. I have an instinctive understanding of cops, who purse their lips and try to hide their anger at the victims as much as at the criminals. It's an unattractive human fact, but a human fact nonetheless.

I have previously given numbers, numbers of dead and numbers of wounded. All such numbers are educated guesses, particularly with respect to the enemy side. I have never heard a report of losses at Singling that made any sense; they all seem too low, much too low. Three hundred 4th Armored men are supposed to have died; I can't·believe it, I *saw* at least two hundred die! Company C lost all its officers, and for a short but crucial time we were commanded by a corporal, a man named DeRosa. Before we reached the gap itself and the nearby city of Strasbourg, however, officer replacements had arrived.

You will notice that neither I nor any other sergeant took command. We didn't want it. DeRosa, lower in rank, was a notable fighter, and when he was offered the command, he quietly accepted it. For the duration of his command, he discharged authority with dignity and firmness. At no time did he say please, but at no time did he allow sudden power to spoil him. The ability to lead men without doting on the fact, the recognition of responsibility without gratuitous ego games, is the mark of a noble warrior. DeRosa was a credit to the 4th Armored Division and therefore one of the great men of World War II. And I don't even know his first name.

The fighting at the gap itself and in and around Strasbourg was something other than a human situation. It was like riding on lightning. The streaking fire did more than merely eradicate the sky, cauterize the earth, and infect the air with an odor of decomposition and sweat. The fire itself infiltrated our heads, so much so that it was like fighting in a state of shock, like trying to shoot through one's own scar tissue. One went through the motions, he loaded his guns, but he wasn't thinking about the battle itself. Nor was he thinking about his home, his wife, his last meal. He simply wasn't thinking.

There was no way to assess the progress of the battle, particularly since the Seventh Army was also playing its vital role—but God knows where, few of us ever actually saw them.

Only later, after the German guns had begun their slow cessation, did we learn that the operation had been successful and the linkup made.

The Germans were like a dying tiger. They were beaten, but, as in all battle, their guns didn't actually fall silent. It was a slow bleeding to death of a tortured dragon, spurts of fire issuing uncontrollably from the mouth that could no longer aim. Was it over? Or were those last gasps merely a preparation for a regrouping? No, it was over, but we had to stay clear of the dying beast, for the trip to Valhalla was a long and lonely one and he wanted company.

But when I realize the strategic factors involved, my jaw slackens. The German high command, particularly Hitler himself, *didn't give a damn about the Belfort Gap!* Their gambit was the Bulge; this was diversion. Stop the Allies if you can, but if not, don't worry; we'll live or die elsewhere—and elsewhere would turn out to be the Ardennes. I remember how in *The Red Badge of Courage* it's eventually revealed that this whole—and again I use the term—epic struggle had been, in the large and inexorable scheme of war, a minor skirmish. But here, at Singling, reality had been so escalated that thousands of human lives were extinguished for something that was of ultimately secondary import. But ultimate pictures and immediate escalations are not necessarily related.

Of the fifteen tanks in my company, nine survived. That's not bad, really. The Germans had not been using that many tanks themselves, so it was therefore more difficult to directly score our machinery. Theirs was an infantry and shell attack, while we had evenly distributed ourselves between man and machine.

No doubt the Germans had not done as much damage as they had wanted. In that sense they were hurt badly, particularly if we assume, and I think we can, that their objective was to render American losses five times greater than their own. That, to second-guess Hitler, would have debilitated the

Third Army's involvement in the Battle of the Bulge. As it turned out, their goals were reversed, and we sat atop the five-to-one advantage.

Had an unmitigated turkey named Thomas Churchill been in charge of the 8th Battalion for any longer than the brief time he was, the Germans might have hurt us. He could barely read a map, let alone assess enemy strengths and positions. We lost dozens of men because of sorties that shouldn't have been made or preparations neglected.

On the other hand, there was a redneck, a Sergeant Luther, who never went to grammar school. His mind *was* a map and his estimates of probable enemy positions and numbers were uncanny. Indeed, Luther received a field commission toward the end of Singling. After the war, however, he couldn't keep it, since he couldn't read. And if you can't read, you can't take tests. And if you can't take tests, you can't lead men. He stayed in the army for the rest of his career, but only as the highest ranking noncom.

Bastogne lay ahead, and then the road to Berlin. But I personally wasn't ready yet. Something had to happen first to jar me back into reality because, like most of the 4th, I was numb, in a state of virtual dissociation. There is a condition common to all wars, which in World War II we called the two-thousand-year stare. This was the anesthetized look, the wide, hollow eyes of a man who no longer cares. I wasn't to that state yet, but the numbness was total. I almost felt as if I hadn't actually been in a battle, as if I had just awakened but couldn't get my body to the bathroom to brush my goddamn teeth. What happened to jar me back to sobriety was one of those small, seemingly insignificant moments that may nonetheless comprise the boundary between sanity and goo-goo time.

A soldier was sitting some fifty yards from my tank. I even remember his face; he had a hooked nose, a small mouth, and bushy eyebrows. He was breathing heavily, panting actually—no doubt he was just tired. And he had a small cut on the left side of his mouth that was bleeding slightly—nothing really, probably cut himself shaving. And yet the sight of him sitting there was like cold water in my face. I was back in the world, or what was left of it. Maybe I needed a small reality, a small pain, to make the big one comprehensible again.

I put my helmet on and climbed back into the tank.

Before Bastogne could happen, before we could cross the Rhine and send Hitler to his bunker, every member of the 4th Armored Division probably had to have some small pain to reconnect him to the inevitable hugeness of war.

# 7

# Purgation

"Nuts!"

A very famous statement. Very famous. Most schoolboys have learned it from their history books, though they probably can't remember exactly who said it or where. The context is too complex for easy understanding; it is even too complex a context for historians to achieve simple agreement. Of course, the historians know who said it, that it was Gen. Anthony MacAuliffe, a deputy to Maxwell Taylor in the 101st Airborne. And they know where he said it. He and his beleaguered men were trapped in a place called Bastogne; Hitler had surprised the Allies with a massive Ardennes counteroffensive against which heroic but insufficiently prepared units like Taylor's stood little chance. But when ordered by the Germans to surrender, MacAuliffe waxed eloquent, if somewhat monosyllabic. Then they had to be rescued, and the counteroffensive stymied. There had to be a Battle of the Bulge.

The agreement ends there, however. I personally admire the refusal to surrender, the mammoth toughness required to wait, fight, and bank on survival. It took balls, which is why MacAuliffe's answer to the Germans had an additional meaning. "Nuts" may have been as much a simple self-description as it was an expression of defiance.

It is nonetheless true that the lives of all those men sweating in their trenches—and there were eventually 652 survivors—were jeopardized. I wonder if that jeopardy was necessary. Had MacAuliffe surrendered, would Hitler have won the Bulge? How important was Bastogne anyway? How much is legend? And how much actual military fact is eclipsed by the swagger of the MacAuliffes and the Pattons?

There are many historians who believe that the real gambit was to the north, at Saint-Vith, where Courtney Hodges's First Army was dealing a mortifying delay to the consolidation of German strength. Some observers might even suggest that Bastogne was pomp and circumstance. According to this view, both sides may have wanted it, but both sides could have lived without it.

In any case, there was nothing pompous or circumstantial about the gallantry of the men themselves, both MacAuliffe's and our own. If Bastogne had been fought in Mozambique three days after armistice, it would still be a vital segment of our history, for ours is a history of sweat. Strategy and tactics, and the personalities of the men who render them, are only important insofar as they make for more or less sweat. With that as our yardstick, nothing is more important than that damn little junction called Bastogne. If MacAuliffe would have been wiser to surrender, the patriotic gore only gets thicker but hardly less relevant. Hell may often be gratuitous, but it's never insignificant.

Just a few words about Hitler's intentions will serve our purposes. In the finest moment of Nazi strategy, Hitler—and I am convinced that Hitler, more than any of his generals, was probably responsible for this masterstroke—decided that an Ardennes push would catch the Allies flatfooted. He was right. Bradley was picking his ass somewhere and would spend the rest of the war smarting from and attempting to obfuscate his own unpreparedness.

Once the initial German breakout was successful, Hitler

would, he hoped, push us back to the Meuse and then aim toward Antwerp. This would completely divide American ground forces and utterly befuddle Allied ambitions. It's unlikely that the German goal here was complete victory. Throughout this period Patton was often saying that the Allies might still lose the war. But that was dissembling on Patton's part, a scare tactic he utilized for leverage against his peers and to keep himself on his toes as well. The fact is, what Hitler wanted to achieve at the Bulge was an option for *conditional* surrender. Remember, in the world of fascist Germany Hitler was a master politician. He could survive a defeat like the one he was hoping for by simply blaming it on someone else. If there were no Jews nor Communists left in Berlin or Munich, he would look elsewhere. That would be second nature to him. The Russian and American armies storming his ramparts, on the other hand, was a totally unacceptable alternative.

As I have noted, Bradley was not ready. American forces were arrayed complacently on a sixty-mile front. Fortunately, the lousy weather and terrain worked to our advantage. If our movement was slow, how much slower were the Germans in their enormous, cumbersome tanks! They thus weren't able to cut up our front enough to beat us. Movement was confined to specific roads, a confinement that made two arterial junctions extremely important: Saint-Vith and Bastogne, the inevitable bottlenecks.

Because of the Third Army's superiority in movement, Patton sensed an opportunity for monumental accomplishment. He couldn't wait; he was licking his chops from breakfast to bed. By December 17, 1944, he had it all figured out—and, in one of the most famous staff meetings in American history, Patton told Eisenhower that he could start for Bastogne immediately and be there by Christmas. Patton's enemies were delighted; he was finally making a complete fool of himself, but he convinced Eisenhower, a man who, despite certain appearances, was not wholly lacking in imagination. Patton had previously wanted to move east from the Saar; the reining order from Bradley had been a severe disappointment. But that disappointment had evaporated now. Ike was giving him carte blanche in something that would be even bigger. The Germans had put their balls on the line, and the Third Army was going to do a bit of stomping.

Speed, speed. Obsessiveness with speed permeated our lives. No one even had to tell us; there were no orders from Patton to move faster. It was understood, it was a given, even if the whole strategic picture was still a bit obscure. We would encounter inclement weather and frozen earth as we neared our destination, but the conditions prevalent at the outset of the run to Bastogne were ideal. Patton thus saw a chance to exploit his superior speed even more fully. Put your fastest men on the fastest ground. He turned to the 4th Armored Division, and we were designated as the vanguard of the Third Army advance.

We started off from Fénétrange, where we had grabbed an additional day or two of rest and regrouping. Within hours we were pushing so hard we were virtually maniacal. It was as if the entire division were performing in a "Roadrunner" cartoon, or as if a 33 LP were being played at 78. We didn't even stop to piss! Individual soldiers would squeeze into the turrets and urinate down the sides of the tanks. Sometimes two men were back to back, their cocks bent over a metallic ridge. An odd phenomenon, as if the tanks themselves were running with yellow sweat! But it only seems weird to me in retrospect. At the time we were so preoccupied with getting to where we wanted to be that it all seemed necessary, and therefore natural.

In two days we encountered enemy artillery fire. This meant that we had arrived; we were there, at the perimeter, at the enemy's south flank, and now we would have to fight as demonically as we had motored if we were to recapture Bastogne and split the German offensive. It was strange, too, the way that initial burst from the enemy scored a tank or two and a few trucks. It seemed as if our forward movement had been so intensive that a kind of irresistible inertia was created whereby we simply couldn't stop, not even to avoid enemy fire. But the Germans weren't throwing everything they had at us. Frankly, I don't think they expected us. Hitler's birthday party was scheduled for midnight, and we were there at noon. Our host wasn't fully dressed yet—though the party promised to be a wild one in any case.

We thus had the chance to reassemble in the vicinity of Arlon. Bastogne itself was sixteen miles away. Some athletes jog sixteen miles every morning and feel all the better for it. But this wasn't Central Park. We were the fastest fighting unit in American history, and it would take us until December 30 to cover those sixteen miles and eradicate enemy resistance. I choose that date as something of a watershed, for it was then that we had a general notion of the costs involved—and that sort of information, so neatly encapsulated and grimly final, has the effect of officially concluding any particular battle. Ninety-six of our vehicles would be in ordnance. Five thousand members of the Third Army would be dead. Thirty-two thousand Germans would join them, more than six times our loss.

I'm getting a bit ahead of myself, however. South of Bastogne, at the base of our sixteen-mile objective, we met some old friends from Brittany, the 5th Para Division. We had crushed them there, and here they were again, reorganized and ready for more. In their own way, these panzer-trained paratroopers were saying "nuts!" to us.

I want to describe these bastards because some observers have underrated them. They were, to be sure, inexperienced, but I can only know that from a later look at relevant documents. The fact is, they didn't act inexperienced. They were slick, savage, continuously shooting, continuously moving forward, almost sullen in their bloody determination. If we beat them, it was only because we were slicker, more savage, more inflexible in fire, movement, persistence.

The initial advantage was theirs. American artillery was an impediment to quick confrontation; our fire, rather than intimidating them and driving them backward, set up a smokescreen behind which they achieved a maximum consolidation. So when we did move forward, they poured hell down our throats. And then German shells came in fast and heavy, considerably more effective than ours had been. The man I called Ernie Jacobson died then, and so did a dozen others. The turrets were hot spots, because 5th Para's gunfire was massive, a sheet of rain spreading like a fan through middle air. Blood, not piss, was running down the sides of our machines. When I remember the Bulge, I remember that the color of movement was yellow, while red was the hue of all immobility.

We were only able to beat them when American aerial and artillery cover threw them back a dozen yards or so. That small German reversal was enough for us; it was like the first inroad we had had in this campaign, and it reawakened some sense of our own invincibility. So we poured it in. We blew out treadings, we exploded gas tanks, we picked off gunners. They were beaten, beaten like heroes; they were beaten but not defeated.

Hardly defeated! Our immediate destination was the town of Burnon. Other detachments were headed for Martelange. From those two vantage points access to Bastogne would be facilitated. But both units of the 4th Armored were delayed. At Martelange a broken bridge proved to be a severe problem, and at Burnon what do we encounter but the rear of the 5th Para!—not as battered as their advance guard had been, but still smarting from a tough setback. Yet there they were, holding us off!

We, the 4th Armored, were supposed to be the experts at rear attack, but if anyone could tarnish our reputation, it was the 5th Para. I don't think they were capable of a simple retreat! Had we ambushed them at any point, they would have whirled around like a tiger; the rear would have become the advance. And at Burnon it fought like the vanguard of the whole Wehrmacht! It amazes me how some critics can give the 4th Armored its just due for the elite unit it was but shrug their shoulders as if the 5th Para were nothing but raw recruits. They were raw, to be sure, but if you don't respect them, you can't possibly respect us, either. Simple amateurs couldn't have given us such hell. There was nothing simple about their amateurism. They were a remarkably valiant band of Germans, maybe the best we saw.

Some of them were on their knees, firing until they died. Others were jumping off burning tanks, pivoting in midair, and shooting as they fell. Still others assembled their tanks and simply refused to budge, firing steadfastly at our forward movement. And when those assemblages of metal burst into flame, the Germans who could survive gathered behind the conflagration and continued firing. I realize now that some of these men were probably getting their first taste of combat— yet these were indistinguishable from those warriors in their ranks who had, perhaps, been at Stalingrad, or Tobruk. It was the only time during the war I ever felt ambivalent about beating the enemy. They were simply too gallant for a man of any sensitivity to destroy without some twinge of bittersweetness.

Burnon was taken, and the 5th Para passed into oblivion. Yet Burnon itself concluded nothing. We were still merely encircling our objective, moving from village to village in narrowing ellipses around Bastogne, like vultures darting from one branch to another toward a supine prey. But our ultimate prey was anything but supine.

Detachments of the 4th Armored occupied Heinstert and Habay-la-Vielle. Bigonville, a town in Luxembourg, was the next significant objective. MacAuliffe's eventual liberator, Creighton Abrams, led his men against it. It was quite a fight, lasting a day and a half. My battalion was simultaneously moving toward Chaumont in what had to be a tactical error. Abrams's men caught hell at Bigonville because the Germans there were ferocious; we, on the other hand, were almost clobbered by pure circumstance and probable misjudgment.

Chaumont was the most glaring failure of Patton's "rock soup method." The essential justification of the use of that tactic at this point was the sunny weather and the effective aerial cover that that sunshine would enable. Thus, any small reconnaissance to Chaumont would be sufficiently protected until Albin Irzyk could bring in the rest of the 8th Tank Battalion; he would also have with him the 10th Armored Infantry, under the sterling command of Harold Cohen.

Everything eventually went as planned, but "eventually" can be a long time. The same sunshine that gave our Thunderbolts a clearer view of the enemy also made mush of the snow and mud. It was an extraordinary mixture, like ice cold oatmeal. As a result, our movement was retarded, excruciatingly so. I was with the initial patrol, and I felt like I had been thrown into a fathomless quicksand.

Notice here the absence of the guiding tactical hand of John Wood. Patton was running us now, for Gaffey was his mouthpiece; and since he was running so many other things as well, he was naturally prone to error. It was the opposite extreme of Robert E. Lee, whose great mistake at Gettysburg was to put too much trust in his subordinates. Patton, on the other hand, barely had subordinates, at least not at this moment. I am convinced that, had Wood still been in power, the whole Chaumont incident would have been radically different and radically easier.

We were thus vulnerable from two standpoints: We in the actual patrol could not move as quickly as we needed to, and the rest of the 8th could not reach us to complete the rock soup ploy with sufficient alacrity. We were sitting ducks, although we did have guns and planes and we used them. And we survived.

It also looked harrowing. Chaumont was a Gothic little

town, and we were approaching it at midnight. It looked like a
black cat curled around itself in the pocket of the dark.
Around fifty farms encircled it—with no life inside, no movement whatsoever, ominous stations, just waiting. Each farm
was fronted by a cylinder of manure, conical formations add-
ing a dreadful symmetry to the scene. And all the while we're
barely moving, all the while we know we're climbing out on a
limb. We weren't stupid. We knew that if we were having trou-
bles, our reinforcements would as well. I thought of George
Cardge, and I wondered how soon I'd be seeing him.

We must have been firing for an hour before the first signs
of our reinforcements appeared. Soon we were a real unit
again, not simply a patrol, but there were still too many of us
bogged down four or five miles behind the fighting line. German fire intensified, and American flesh began to crackle and
stink. We withdrew under monumental shelling and bazooka
fire, pulling back some of our reinforcements with us as we
retreated. This was the first withdrawal I had experienced
since Rennes, and it felt even more bitter—for here I knew that
it was because of terrain and of our own miscalculations
rather than of German resistance. If a better soldier beats me,
he beats me. I can live with that. And at least at Rennes we
were able to plunge right back in. Here at Chaumont I had
more the feeling it was a general rout, and, believe me, I
hated it!

American forces had been hit at every point of contact
with Chaumont's defenders. There is a well-known story that
derives from this withdrawal. As we were pulling back, a tank
drove past a ditch in which sat an American soldier, quietly
and patiently, without the least trace of physical anguish or
mental despair in his manner. He could have been reading the
Sunday papers. The man in the turret stared down at him,
speechless. The soldier looked up and smiled and called out
jovially, "Hi-ya fellas!" The only unusual thing about him was
that his foot had been completely shot off, and veins were
dangling from the end of his ankle.

As the 35th got itself together and managed to secure

Martelange, the last of the 8th reinforced us, and we pushed back into Chaumont. My respect for Albin Irzyk skyrocketed at this point. He could sense that this was now no "rolling eight ball," that here we would have to muster up our moral courage as well as our physical strength. His attitude throughout was one of quiet encouragement—no Knute Rockne bullshit—and sympathetic understanding of the mind of the soldier edging precariously toward defeat. He didn't slap any of us. None of us deserved it. He simply assessed a situation, reorganized it, and encouraged us back to victory.

With the arrival of the last of the rock soup increments, the tide of Chaumont flowed our way. Our line was solidified, and German resistance was not as strong as it had been; they too had suffered their losses, and each one of the enemy had been involved in the thick of fighting. We, on the other hand, were coming in with soldiers who had not seen actual fire in a day or two. That freshness won the battle. German resistance buckled and vacillated and then fell. What is notable is the effectiveness of the "rock soup method" even at its worst, even at a moment when it probably shouldn't have been used. The fact is, the ready availability of fresh men will inevitably win a fight for you. Our problem at Chaumont had merely been to survive until they arrived. The American miscalculation had therefore been one of time and distance; the availability had not been ready enough.

When it was all over and Chaumont was ours, eleven American tanks had been destroyed. Eerily enough, that was the precise number we lost at Rennes. I haven't trusted that number since; I associate it with the precipice. But others had it worse. An entire infantry company had been wiped out, and every officer in it was dead. An especially fine lieutenant named William Patton, a quiet, courageous man from Virginia whom I had met between bouts in France, was killed while searching for an escape route for his trapped unit. Again I think of Rennes, the one place where I too had been trapped. I suppose that claustrophobia inevitably goes with defeat. I wondered how many German soldiers had sufferred nervous breakdowns during their disastrous evacuations in Brittany. Claustrophobia ain't good! Indeed, defeat demands its own kind of discipline, just as victory does.

As costly as Chaumont was, as tough as the 5th Para had been, as exasperating as donnybrooks like Martelange were for other units of the 4th Armored, the central gauntlet was yet to be run. The extraordinary 37th now pushed off from Bigonville and took a handful of crucial little towns; their movements utterly surprised German resistance. Then the 4th Armored fanned out in two directions. Half of us concentrated in the area just north of Grandrue, while the other half took Hallange and consolidated itself there. Grandrue and Hallange: I don't think they're on most historians' maps, and it's possible that Patton and Gaffey would barely remember them. But to the dog soldier they were points of reorganization, psychic reorganization if nothing else! That alone gives them inestimatable value. And if a Hallange saves the average soldier's mind, then it becomes as tactically important as Bastogne itself.

Our infantry took the town of Remoiville, and devastated it. It was assumed that German stragglers were gathering there and that other enemy units may have been reassembling in the vicinity. So we took no chances. Each house on each block was cleared with a flamethrower; each set of windows was washed out with fire. It was an operation almost grotesque in its systematic elaboration. And beyond Remoiville lay a single road. That road began in Martelange. It was covered on each side with evergreens, no doubt a very idyllic drive in peacetime. The 4th Armored barreled down that road with all the speed it could muster, its full strength marshaled in double columns where possible but more often in a serpentine single file. The day before I had said my prayers in Chaumont. Today it was sunset, then night, and I was alone in my turret, wary, peering down this narrow gravel road that led directly to a man named MacAuliffe and his 652 subordinates.

Many of us would not finish the drive that led there. On each side of the road, hidden in the dark green of the Melch Woods, were crackling bazookas; some of them were alone—enterprisingly piratical snipers—while others were grouped in threes and fours, their rapid fire piercing the moonless night with flat discordances.

We poured intensive fire into the woods as we drove. There's no way of telling how many snipers we got, but I would guess most of them. Anytime a bazooka picked at us, frequently causing mechanical and human loss, at least four or five tanks would unleash their guns in that direction. Only a mole could have survived.

Indeed, there were a considerable number of Germans flushed out of the Melch Woods and still others wandering aimlessly on the road—men who were, no doubt, completely lost and simply too sick and tired and hungry to care who found them first. Many of them we simply left; we had no time to worry about prisoners. Still others ran or attempted—almost in delirium—to fire at us; these we killed.

As we neared the towns of Remichampagne and Bois de Cohet, however, the action intensified once again, and there were simply too many prisoners to release. Many of these Germans were determined to break out after we had taken them into custody; they attacked our MPs, almost as if they were inviting death. Not one German escaped, and not one American MP was killed. Soon the 35th, which was driving on a road that had forked to the opposite side of the woods, was firing incessantly, as if prisoners and snipers had singled them out for resistance. Bad choice—the 35th didn't stop moving, not for a second.

Our artillery support increased. That was a harmony I didn't mind listening to, however atonal. They blasted all hell out of Bois de Cohet, and German soldiers fled it like stallions from a burning barn. There were three fugitives who will remain in my consciousness until the day I die. One was a German soldier standing by the edge of the woods. His feet were bare and beside him were three pairs of shoes. A man from my tank jumped down to get him. Without so much as looking at his captor, the German tried on one pair of shoes, muttered something incoherent, and kicked them off. Then the second pair. His toes protruded and he took those off, too. Finally, the third pair—which seemed all right to me, but what the hell do I know! Once again he took off the shoes, and then collapsed. My comrade peered down at him and returned to the tank. "He's dead," he told me.

It wasn't twenty minutes later that I saw two Germans running along the outer base of the evergreens, one man some fifty yards behind the other. They both had guns in their hands. "Halt!" I shouted, but they continued running. I fired above the lead man's head, and when he still wouldn't stop, I began to take aim. But the man whirled around and pointed his gun at the German behind him—not fast enough! The man behind him fired three times, killing his countryman. Then he flung his gun away and surrendered.

Everyone who had seen it tried to question the man later. No response. Name, rank, serial number. And then we stopped trying. The look on the man's face was frightening; there was something so desolate about him, and yet that desolation expressed itself in terms of pure meanness. We just got rid of him as quickly as we could. What had it been? A woman?—no, love and sex could never have inspired such a face. Politics?— maybe. Maybe one of the men had decided that Adolf Hitler was no damn good, and that decision had tended to cause a bit of friction between the two. Or maybe—and I can't get this thought out of my mind—maybe they were brothers. . . .

As our aerial and artillery cover increased, so did our speed. We were impeded now only by the necessity of dealing with larger and larger numbers of prisoners. But sniper fire decreased, and you could feel the self-confidence of the division rising like lava. It was up to MacAuliffe now. If he could hold out, we'd get to him.

There were still German-held towns in our path, but the nightmare of Chaumont now seemed to belong to another war. At Remichampagne the 8th Battalion had its finest moment. We came up east of the town, and the antitank response was enormous. But we just outran the fire. Our movement was so savage that it would have been fatuous for the Germans to have taken any aim. They could only fire and hope; we were blowing them out in a continuous barrage.

If there was one moment at Remichampagne that typified the way we fought, it was the performance of Sgt. Frank Gill and Cpl. Mike Cotus, whose valor added a permanent footnote to the history of the 4th Armored. Their tank was caught on the outskirts of the town by an .88 antitank gun that seemed to have found its range. Two rounds struck the tank itself and almost destroyed it; a light, rather than a medium, tank would have exploded. Other rounds, no doubt from the same gun, were landing around them. Gill and Cotus did the logical thing. They crawled out of the tank and went looking for the gun that was causing them the problem. On their bellies they crawled, through shells and bazookas, until they spotted it—and then back the same unspectacular, methodical way to their tank. They knew where they had been, they knew where the offending weapon was, so what else to do but blow it away!

Two more hamlets, Clochimont and Assenois! We were south of Clochimont, three miles from the rendezvous at Bastogne. American cargo planes dotted the sky; they'd be bringing us the supplies to take to MacAuliffe. But German antiaircraft fire was not to be discounted. The sky ignited with alabaster flak. One cargo was hit; it sailed smoothly through the atmosphere until it glided down a thousand feet or so. Now it was whirling and twitching in a death spasm; it crashed in a narrow funnel of flame that shot back down as fast as it had risen. But once that thin passage of fire subsided, it exploded latitudinally, and soon there was nothing left of the plane but its skeleton. Nothing could be salvaged.

We stayed at Clochimont to organize our line and facilitate the transfer of supplies. I would personally get no closer to Bastogne than this—which was fine with me. There had already been glory enough, and there would be more in the days ahead. I am, in retrospect, satisfied that it was the 4th Armored that did eventually rescue MacAuliffe rather than any other unit of the Third Army. We had, after all, been the vanguard; we had cleared the path from Alsace-Lorrain to the Ardennes. If Bastogne is strategically overrated, it was still a massive accomplishment for any individual dog soldier to have arrived there; the human triumph was greater than any military factor could possibly be. If anything is unfair, it is the sorry negligence that popular "wisdom" has afforded General Hodge and the men of the First Army, whose heroism at Saint-Vith was certainly the equal of ours further south.

The triumph of relieving MacAuliffe would fall to a man and to a battalion that certainly deserved it: Creighton Abrams and the 37th, in concert with the 53rd Infantry. But there was still fighting to be done between Clochimont and Bastogne; Abrams still had to take the village of Assenois. It was a gruesome last-ditch effort by the Germans. Like the 5th Para, these Germans simply refused to fall-back; they were a final stonewall in which each block of granite preferred utter demolition to collapse. Indeed, that sums up the German effort in the Ardennes. At the outset I saw the 5th Para, who had fought like gods—and, as if to complete a circle, the 37th encountered a legion at Assenois that strove the same way, except these gods knew their twilight was at hand.

It was also Assenois that saw one of the greatest feats of individual daring in the history of the 4th Armored. A private named James Hendrix, who was the very definition of a redneck, earned decorations on three counts, three very long counts. The first feat that young gentleman performed was to single-handedly knock out an .88. How? Well, he charged the gun on foot! Hurling himself over the ridge, he shot one of the gunners in the neck and pistol-whipped the other.

That was just the first count. After he caught his breath, he saved a number of men who were lying wounded just beneath the sights of a German machine gun. Hendrix leaped from his tank, lifted his rifle, and simply whaled away at the enemy until the wounded were evacuated. Oh, and he finished off the day by racing across mines and crossfire, jumping into a burning tank, and pulling out the trapped man within. That man eventually died from his burns, but Hendrix was the kind of guy who would have done it anyway, even had he been able to foresee the man's fate. Hendrix was one of the few soldiers who ever actually did what the Alvin Yorks and the Audie Murphys are supposed to have done.

Abrams's men took Assenois, they did a little more driving, and then they made it. Made what? Made 652 men very, very happy! MacAuliffe had delivered on his immortal monosyllable—with, of course, a little help from his companions, who would now be known everywhere as the battered bastards of Bastogne. That first moment of contact is one that's always worth recounting. A Lieutenant Boggess it was who first spotted the signs of supplies in an open field, articles that indicated the presence of American soldiers. "Come on out," he called. No response. "This is the 4th Armored." Still nothing.

Finally a rustle of movement. An officer named Webster stood up, slowly, suspiciously. Then he smiled and strode forward. "Glad to see you," he said. A few minutes later MacAuliffe, representing Maxwell Taylor, made it official by shaking hands with Creighton Abrams. It was December 26. Patton had promised Ike it would be Christmas—and half the Allied command had laughed! Well, they were right. He was one day late!

Again, however, I feel obliged to reemphasize the extraordinary role played by the First Army to our north. Whatever glory we of the Third achieved at Bastogne may well have been precluded by the kind of breakout at Saint-Vith the Germans had planned on. Had that happened, there may not have been a MacAuliffe left to rescue. We are speaking really of five days. History shows that the Germans wanted Saint-Vith by the seventeenth; they didn't get it until the twenty-second. Five days in war is more than simply crucial; in the Battle of the Bulge it proved to be the equivalent of nine innings—particularly since the American push from the south was conceptually based on celerity of movement. Had General Hodge been a less retiring man, had he known as much about newspapers as he did about war, he would surely have gained the recognition out of which he's been so tragically cheated.

Had the First not held Saint-Vith, the Third Army may have been cooked, however tough and valiant its campaign. In an odd twist, then, they rescued us, the rescuers of MacAuliffe. This would also suggest that the Germans saw Bastogne as immediately expendable—for by linking up their forces with the panzers coming down from Saint-Vith, they would have recaptured it anyway. If this was indeed their attitude, it puts the defenders of Chaumont and Assenois, not to mention the 5th Para, in an odd light, for they fought so fiercely, so desperately, and they died in such heavy numbers, and for what?—for only the second most important segment of the Battle of the Bulge. Of course, this tendency toward sacrifice for a less than ultimately important goal was not unusual for the Germans; we saw it before in the Battle of Singling and the struggle for the Belfort Gap. It was thus a very paradoxical desperation that gave Singling its epic proportion and Bastogne its legendary reputation.

Yet even if we accept the fact that the First Army at Saint-Vith made our achievement at Bastogne possible, additional glory redounds to the 4th Armored, for there is a magnificent irony contained in all of this. The center of the Saint-Vith junction was defended by a unit of the First Army commanded by Bruce Clark. And Bruce Clark was a 4th Armored original——trained by John Wood and tested by some of the same fire that had tested me. It is notable how many officers came from the 4th Armored, how many men had been guided toward power by John Wood. No, Wood was gone by the time of Bastogne, but even here his hand reached out to play no small part in one of our greatest glories. He made it possible for us to guarantee ourselves rescue by one man so we could rescue another. History, saith the poet, has many cunning corridors.

Bastogne was, finally, the greatest moment in our history for quotes. If John Paul Jones said, "I have not yet begun to fight"; if Oliver Hazard Perry said, "We have met the enemy, and they are ours"; and if James Lawrence said, "Don't give up the ship"—then Jones and Perry and Lawrence were pompous assholes! I'll take "Nuts!" any day. Even Patton is on record for praising MacAuliffe's eloquence, and I can only second that record enthusiastically. It was the next to greatest line in American military history.

The greatest line, and a line it was, also occurred during the Bulge, though it came a bit later than MacAuliffe's, from a 4th Armored man racing to rescue the "Nuts!" man. In his book on Patton, Ladislas Farago quotes an anonymous GI as having said, "So they got us surrounded again, the poor bastards!" I would like to give a very substantial identity to that anonymity. His name was Constant Klinga, a noncom, a joker, a swaggerer, a fucker if not a lover, a great Dodgers fan, an occasional drinker, a man no writer—not even Brendan Behan—could invent. The quality of most officers is, in part, dependent on the extent to which they share the common character of their men. MacAuliffe and Klinga have much in common. How great, how natural their utterances were!—and how contrived, how rhetorical John Paul Jones seems in comparison. I knew Klinga well, and I'd like to have known MacAuliffe.

There was still a little more to come. The fact that the Germans were finished actually served to prolong the Battle of the Bulge. Bastogne was now more important than it had ever been because Patton and the rest of the Allies would use it as an offensive springboard. So the Germans had to try to get it back, and the fighting enflamed again in a savage enemy counterattack that centered in and around the village of Lutrebois. Later I would hear something about that battle that astounds me to this day. The most ferocious German fighting at Lutrebois was done by remnants of the 5th Para! No comment!

But no matter how ferocious the German counterattack had been, they would have lost! We had been so well supplied after the rescue, and our confidence was at such a peak, that the enemy might as well have tried to extinguish the sun with a rubber hose. They lost fifty-five tanks at Lutrebois; that's well over twice our combined tank loss at Chaumont and Rennes. And from December 3, 1944, to January 6, 1945, we poured the rattle of twenty-five thousand howitzers into that doomed little town. American fire practically razed the timber around Lutrebois; not too many stragglers would escape that battle.

Then came a setback of sorts. The Germans were retreating through a town called Houffalize, which functioned as a kind of bottleneck. It was extremely well defended; the Germans were ready for an attack. But Bradley wanted Houffalize. Well, the 4th Armored and the 101st Airborne took it by the end of the month, but it was an inch-by inch proposition. Patton didn't like the whole damn thing any more than his men did, not when American losses were piling up and only two miles had been gained. But the orders were intractable, and the town was eventually secured.

Houffalize did, at least, serve as an effective point from which we could push further into the Bulge. If the fight for

Bastogne proper had concluded by the end of 1944, the Battle of the Bulge itself, and all that that implied, officially ended by February 1945. But history hadn't ended yet, and neither had World War II. Ahead of us lay the Siegfried Line, or West Wall, the classic German defense that ran from Cleves to the Swiss border. A new campaign was about to begin. But I had the right to get laid first. We rested in Luxembourg, if *rested* is the right word. There was plentiful wine, and the women even spoke English.

We pushed off from Bettendorf. Now, the Siegfried Line, which was our natural objective, was encased in a conundrum of rivers. Each river was a natural defense; the play of one against another rendered the terrain innately formidable. There was the Our, the Sauer, the Moselle again, the Saar, and the Gay. The Gay flowed back into the Sauer. To the east were the Enzbach and the Nims, and the Prüm. This entire network was enclosed to the east by the vital Kyll—and the Kyll in turn flowed into the Moselle. It was one of those puzzles in which smaller boxes are always popping out of bigger ones. We would have to pick the best place to start, hopefully the point at which the spider was least protected by the labyrinth nature had given him. The hinge of the Sauer and the Moselle was selected, a fortunate choice.

Detachments of the 4th Armored blew their way into Germany at Ferschweiller, denting the West Wall and penetrating Hitler's iron chastity belt. His violators were the 5th Infantry attached to 4th Armored. Beyond Ferschweiller lay Sinspelt, where victory would smash the Siegfried Line. To attain that objective, the first major movement of 4th Armored men crossed the Sauer and secured the town of Dillengen. Another unit of the 4th, which included my 8th Battalion, drove a relentless forty miles to Lahr, Germany. Small pockets of enemy resistance fled before our advance, firing as they fled. I wonder how those Germans felt; for the first time, they were being beaten on German soil. Yet their faces looked no different from the other defeated faces I had seen, at Singling, near Bastogne, in Brittany. Defeat is bitter more from a personal standpoint; you feel as if, after so many years of watching your brothers die, it had all been in vain. In other words, you haven't been merely beaten, like the 5th Para. You've been *defeated*. Defeated: that word is so resonant with so many awful dimensions of emotion. And, if that word is reverberating in your head with all its dreadful timbre, the last thing you'll worry about is whose soil you happen to be standing on. Patriotism has driven many men to many deeds, but in the last apocalyptic moment it proves of no vital concern.

In one sense, the enigma of rivers protecting the West Wall worked to our advantage. The Germans were relying much too heavily on these natural obstacles. They had skimped on mines, on blockhouses, on pillboxes. There was really no excuse for such a blunder. You can't count on anything, not even an erupting volcano, to stop the advance of a notoriously fast army and division, especially a rested one—especially one that's just come off the exhilaration of an Ardennes triumph and smells more blood ahead. No, they should have thrown everything they had at us.

The eventual American victory was a strong one, and gave great promise to the whole push into Germany that was just beginning. Company A of my battalion destroyed eight tanks along the road to Sinspelt. It was an extraordinary maneuver, a kind of semicircle designed to net all eight, to prevent access to Sinspelt by any one of them. As a result, the town itself could now only be defended by infantry and stragglers. And that proved to be a sorry, desperate defense, for, after obliterating all eight of the approaching panzers, Company A seized the bridge along the Enzbach that afforded Sinspelt its only lifeline.

We approached the Prüm and seized the town of Brecht. The retreating Germans were more competent here and blew out the bridge across the river. There was nothing to capture. Shit,

I could hear a nearby lieutenant mutter, shit, shit, shit. But the delay was a brief one. We bridged the river as few rivers have ever been bridged. Seven or eight of us returned to our tanks and aimed our guns at the bases of a string of telephone poles. They fell like matchsticks. Then a score of men started rolling them toward the river bank. Others waded on ahead and caught them as they tumbled in. A plainlike raft was established, not the sturdiest in the world but sturdy enough to afford us a bridgehead. We wouldn't have to wait for the more circumspect operations of our engineers.

No, nothing was going to stop us now—nothing except the orders of our own superiors, which were to wait at the Kyll for mop-up operations to commence and conclude. The hiatus was agonizing. We were so close to the Rhine, so restless. In a sense, we felt that to stop now would be to lose momentum, delay the war, and decrease our maximum efficiency. And that would cost lives, although, as it turned out, there was no diminution in either momentum or effectiveness—and the Rhine would soon be ours. In the meantime, other units of the 4th Armored were capturing the vital town of Rittersdorf. Rittersdorf and one thousand prisoners!

The Americans had come up on the town so fast that the Germans had had no choice but to abandon their rear guards. And those rear guards added up; unlike the prisoners taken at Remichampagne during the run to Bastogne, these men were too smart to be desperate. They simply surrendered, while their vanguards retreated across the Nims and settled along those spots by the Kyll still untaken by our advance. There was plenty of time now for consolidation; we were reequipped with every variety of weapon, and ammunition trucks were coming up by the dozen. Then more good news: The First Army had taken Cologne.

Blood. We smelled blood.

The ultimate leg was about to begin, for the Rhine was dead ahead. If our speed held out, if we could duplicate our feat at

Bastogne, the war would end that much sooner, and thousands of lives would be saved. We moved from our spot at the Kyll and took up a station at Bitburg, where the last preparations were to be made. Bitburg was a ruined village, all rubble and blood. This fact added, I feel now, a final symbolic dimension to our last great push. It was as if we were rising from the ashes, phoenixlike, to attack the final night, and thereby hasten the new day. And at the same time, those ashes of Bitburg served as a fitting representation of all the decimation we had previously encountered and caused.

We drove north along the Kyll, then swung east. Our plan was to follow the Moselle until it met the Rhine—again, the Moselle was serving as a powerful watershed in the history of the 4th Armored. Our speed at this time was the stuff of fable; to say that we were incredible is a mere exercise of fact, not braggadocio. What made it even more remarkable was the fog, the opaque fog, and the incessant rain, muddying up the already difficult ground. Fifty-eight hours, and we made our destination, the town of Koblenz; the fact is, 158 hours would have been more likely.

In addition, the fog made aerial cover useless. We were consequently as vulnerable to ambush as we were to the troublesome weather. By the seventh or eighth hour of the journey, however, we were firing at unseen snipers with almost unconscious movement. Our minds were singularly intent on the next mile ahead, and the next. The presence of individual Germans, your own would-be assassins, was no more preoccupying to us than a broken-down barn on a cross-country drive. We simply fired their way with lazy abstraction. But we never stopped moving.

The rain rendered the roads well-nigh impassable—and certainly inaccessible to any double file of tanks. What ultimately emerged was a single file consisting of the entire 4th Armored Division on one road. Again, circumstance was contributing lustrous symbolic weight to the moment. We were all together: the best at their best, preparing to climax the second world war in a century. It was almost as if we were parading ceremoniously, in a last manifestation of our full strength, of our consummate identity—a final show, for the benefit of anyone who could see, of human strength stretched to the very limits of the human. Except there was no one there to see.

Sixty-five miles. Sixty-five miles to Koblenz. And fifty-eight hours . . .

Within twenty hours we were taking prisoners, but what prisoners! The Germans were hurting. We captured at least six woodchoppers, and about a dozen men who eventually admitted that this had been the first time they had ever held guns in their hands. Their normal implements were shovels. And they kept coming, hundreds of them, and surrendering with nothing more than token resistance. We had our double columns back, except now our tanks weren't "married up" to each other but to a seemingly interminable stream of German extras.

By now the phrase "Roosevelt's butchers" could hardly sum up the German attitude toward us. We began to use psychological warfare, a technique for which one Alexis Sommaripa developed a small reputation. Oh, but this was no Tokyo Rose spiel Alexis used, nor was it anything akin to totalitarian brainwashing. It was a very simple and honest method. "This is the Fourth Armored Division," Alexis would call out on a megaphone. "You can't see us and we can't see you, but eventually we'll find you. If you don't care to engage the Fourth Armored in battle, surrender now!"

And they did, scores of them. Alexis would finish his pitch, and then there would be a pause, a rustle, then a volley of frightened calls, usually in German but sometimes in broken English. Like the dead on Judgment Day, they emerged from unmitigated dark and begged for mercy.

As we neared Koblenz, Alexis was less useful, for the presence of German tanks was an ever-increasing phenomenon. We saw a whole column heading for Koblenz, and we blitzed it. Rather than hold their ground, they fired back at us as they increased their fugitive speed, sighting the distant town like an oasis in the desert. But they didn't make it. Not one of them.

The 8th Battalion found and secured the hamlets of Karlich and Muhlheim while other units of the 4th finished off the few remaining panzers, for whom Koblenz was now but a dream. By the time we assembled in Koblenz, the 4th Armored Division was further east than any other American unit. Our achievement left everyone, Allied and Axis alike, somewhat stunned. And what had we lost? Twenty-nine men, just twenty-nine men it took to violate the wickedest land of all.

We waited. In a tactical retreat German forces attempted to cross the Rhine at Urmitz and thereby establish a strong defense on the other side. But they didn't make that, either. We raced to the Urmitz crossing and blew the bridge, shattering the enemy maneuver. They pulled back in chaos and were mopped up. You'll notice, however, that none of us had yet crossed the Rhine. No, not yet. The Germans still had considerable pockets of men and force on the western side, of which the detachment that had attempted Urmitz was but the advance guard. The others would have to be destroyed first, and we'd have to track them down, in an area known as the Palatinate Triangle, a dense ground formed between the Moselle, the Rhine, and the Saar.

But beyond that . . .

# 8

# Beethoven's Shame

The Germans were applying their own psychological warfare as we approached the Palatinate. The route was littered with large cardboard placards warning us of the American defeat that lay ahead. These were, to my knowledge of the European war, unique to the Palatinate. "Stop!" said one, "Death Is Ahead." Another one read, "This Is Our Ballpark Now," a worthy effort, to be sure, to communicate with the enemy in his own vernacular. The funniest one was a five- or six-foot rhomboid sign on which was printed, in oversized, shockingly red letters, the simple words, "You Will Bleed!"

Sometimes we shot them down as we drove, most of the time we just laughed and went past. It was, in the main, a rather paltry effort. We knew the Germans were beat, and no nativity of soil would reverse the tidal wave of American progress. Indeed, the fact that the enemy would warn us against our own eventual destruction—such a patently absurd suggestion—actually worked against them; they were only reminding us of how inevitable our victory was. In that sense this propaganda effort boosted rather than demoralized our spirits.

Yet there was a slight truth to the German bullshit. It didn't really matter that the Americans had it all in the bag; these signs could have been true, *were true*, for some of us. We could have been charging a cancer ward, but if moribund men have guns and tanks and shells, some healthy men will surely die. "You Will Bleed" was true, not for the American army, but for some small percentage of it—and we knew that when we read the sign, we knew it as we laughed. The only thing we didn't know were the names comprising the *you* in "You Will Bleed." So I'd be less than honest if I said that these German efforts were wholly ineffective; there were twinges of fear, taciturn comprehensions of the abyss, somewhere beneath the surface of our self-assured derision.

I wonder, though, what the Germans would have done had they been able to foresee the eventual outcome of the Palatinate campaign. From the moment we moved from Koblenz to the moment we actually crossed the Rhine, thirty-seven thousand Germans would die! It would be one of our most facile and significant adventures, and one of the fastest! The Rhine would be closed from Koblenz all the way to Mannheim. Enormous sources of coal and steel would be lost to the Reich; not only would this cripple the enemy's staying power in general, but it would also mitigate continuous panzer resistance and confrontation. And that made me feel a lot better. The Palatinate would be the embalming fluid for the corpse that was accomplished at the Bulge—and it would take a mere three or four days to inject.

We took the town of Pfeddersheim to our west. German resistance was inconsiderable; a few units stood their ground just outside the town, but we went through them like butter. They scattered north and south, and then probably fell back behind Pfeddersheim, hoping to link up with the main German "line." I doubt they made it. Inside the village we were greeted by a number of townspeople frantically trying to convince us of their friendship. Enormous white sheets and towels were being waved from the windows; they flutterred in the breeze like flags, but the town looked more like Delancey

Street on laundry day. One woman leaned out of a top story window and exposed her breasts; she was telling us how much she loved us and how little she wanted to die. If you couldn't get laid in Germany, you couldn't get laid in a whorehouse! Yet we would still hear an occasional story about an American soldier who actually saw the need to rape a civilian. These men were always arrested and often shot. They deserved it.

If the puny German efforts at propaganda had, at the very least, added a slightly unnerving edge to the Palatinate, the progress of the campaign assuaged it; in fact, by the time we took the village of Pfiffligheim (just read it, don't pronounce it), the campaign was dominated by a mood of great good humor. Pfiffligheim itself was cake; as soon as we started firing, German soldiers dashed out of the town and literally raced into the arms of Allied captivity.

There were Germans, however, still cowering around the buildings at the edge of town; they weren't resisting, they weren't shooting, they were just cowering and letting us do the work of capturing them. Bob Saville, myself, and two or three others, left our tanks to get them. They came out willingly. Bob had an enormous problem, however. There was a phrase we all used when the task at hand was rounding up German stragglers. As best as I can transliterate, we'd shout "Dropen zee der waffen und comin' zee out mit der hant heuch!" For some reason Bob had never used this phrase before; he had not personally taken many prisoners, and the ones he had had surrendered so willingly he had never been forced to try out his pidgin German.

Three enemy privates were standing in the shadow formed by the eaves of a small tavern just within the village. Bob whipped up his rifle and said, in a clear, ringing voice, "Dop zee voich und mitterdoo!" Nothing. The Germans didn't move. He shouted with greater insistence. "Und zee dope your hoy hoy!" The Germans walked forward a pace or two but only to examine this odd American; they screwed up their eyes and peered at him like a man glaring, with no small discomfort, at a peep show that features a sex act he's never even heard of, let alone seen. But Bob wasn't going to shoot them; he looked to me for help.

"Just tell them to drop their hoy hoy," I said.

"Fuck you," said Bob, and turning to the Germans once again, he shouted, "Give up, goddammit!" And then they did.

Bob Saville was a clown, like Klinga or Cronan. But Bob was not pure clown; he was that magnificent hybrid of clown and hero that the American army, perhaps more than any other, has always grown in such blessed abundance. I have seen Bob Saville in a turret, blasting away, his face registering the fear, or, more precisely, the certain knowledge of imminent death— and I never saw him relent. A man who is not afraid to die earns no heroism in his relentlessness. Like every other man I ever respected, Bob wanted to live; he loved life like the juiciest little plum but never fled the circumstances that threatened to rot the tree and desiccate the fruit. And he would survive.

We approached and captured the historic town of Worms, our entry into which gave some soldier an opportunity for a devastatingly cruel prank. As we drove through the streets, the humanity of the town stuck its head out of its windows, while a few others ambled guardedly onto the curb. Then somebody in our ranks cried, "Russki! Russki!" You should have seen those shutters slam closed; the handful who had adventured the street turned on their heels and wouldn't stop running. God, how Goebbels had made them fear the Russians! All of the townspeople's most private and perverse sadomasochistic fantasies were given the looming shape of potential reality by the thought of the Russian army turned loose in their backyards to rape and dismember and disembowel.

The fact, of course, that it was Goebbels who had made them fear the Russians did not, in and of itself, render those fears irrational. I said earlier that really great liars like

Goebbels always begin with a kernel of truth. The rapine viciousness of the Red Army was just such a kernel. And who could blame the Reds after what the Germans had done to their wives and brothers? It is almost a tribute to Russian humanity that they simply didn't cannibalize every German they saw.

But the German citizens of Worms were innocent of all that. They simply wanted to see American flesh and avoid the almost certain searing of their flesh by Stalin's angry legions. It must have taken our detachments a month to finally mollify the city's great and now all-pervasive terror. At any rate we had ourselves another historic site to add to Orléans and Metz.

Just beyond Worms a large division of Germans was attempting to evacuate across the Rhine and ensconce themselves deeper into the now chimerical security of Germany. They didn't make it; most of them died trying. There were seventy or eighty rowboats floating in the river, having been originally earmarked for the east bank. They were all manned by corpses, shot-up bodies entwined around the oars, hanging over the sides, reclining peacefully. It made for an eerie sight: the dead carrying the dead. Some of the boats were sinking slowly, littering this ultimate German river with the decomposition of German flesh. Others had not been punctured at all. They continued to float like the bullrushes that carried Moses to survival, but now the cargo was a dead cargo and would bear no future savior of the German people.

Yet most of the Germans who died outside Worms never made it to a rowboat. They were trapped at the river bank, awaiting a boat that wouldn't have done them any good anyhow. They fell on rich mud, they slipped, splashing, into the murky pockets where water meets earth. It was impossible to take many prisoners, for the ones who continued to try to flee were mixed inextricably with the ones who simply wanted to reach an American and give up. We had no choice but to fire at all of them.

But at least two hundred of these Germans would survive,

thanks to Paul Glaz. His tank was well ahead of the others in our company; he must have been one hundred yards closer to the river. Around fifty Germans approached him with their hands held high; some one hundred and fifty others were behind them, still making for the Rhine. He ordered his gunner to sight and hold the ones who were surrendering; then from the turret he fired on ahead of the ones who were in flight. Maybe one or two were injured. He increased his fire and the whole damn brigade halted, as if it were one collective mechanism whose switch had been turned off.

Paul drove around the column without taking his weapons off a single man. He reached the front and ordered the whole unit backward—and backward they went, their ranks an odd mixture of fear and relief. He delivered all two-hundred to our rear and then returned. Well, such a combination of guts and brains deserves some commendation because we never had enough men or enough time to properly handle the capture and delivery of enemy soldiers.

Yet our attack across the Rhine would not follow immediate suit. All of the natural and man-made access points across the Rhine at Worms were either decimated or inoperative. This was no great setback. We approached the Rhine by crossing the Moselle again—for the third time. That river was beginning to feel like my bathtub.

Once over the Moselle, we found ourselves hot on the tail of the enemy in the Hunsruck Mountains. True to form, we tore up their rear. Twelve hundred of them surrendered and were hustled quickly westward. By the middle of March we had taken Bad Kreuznach, a spa.

It was just outside Bad Kreuznach that the Germans delivered their last counteroffensive before we crossed the Rhine; they still wanted a path across the river and weren't going to give it up easily. The fighting was intense, uncharacteristically so for the Palatinate episode. Their panzers seemed fresh, and so did the men—God knows how!

If my friend Paul Glaz had distinguished himself a day or so earlier, it was now Andy Cammerrary's turn. He was surrounded by two panzers and half a dozen German infantrymen, who had somehow barreled past the front line of the American defense. He told me later he gave himself up for dead then, and yet all he could remember was being pissed off that he would die during such an easy American campaign. Not that other Americans weren't getting killed, but there was something fluky about dying here, as if, in contrast to the Bulge or Avranches or Singling, it could only happen in an accident.

Paradoxically enough, that pissed-off attitude probably saved Andy's life. He worked his adrenalin up and drove back the infantrymen. Then he saw one of the German tanks go up in flame; something had hit it, perhaps a German shell, perhaps an American tank on Andy's blind side. He whirled his machine around some twenty degrees and started blowing at the other panzer, backing up as he fired. Then the panzer's treading skipped, like a conveyor belt ungluing. The German threw himself into reverse, panicking, no doubt, and skidded over altogether. He had missed his chance to surrender. Of course Andy had not had that option. He could see the other American machines moving further on. He didn't want to be left behind—so when a German soldier rolled out of his smashed turret, Andy shot him. And then he caught up to the rest of us.

"Fuckin' thing," Andy murmured to me later on, shaking his head.

"Andy," I said, "you're a pro."

Now it was time. We went over the Rhine at Oppenheim in a steady rolling thunder of 4th Armored men and machines that wound across from early evening of March 24 to the next morning. March 25, 1945, it was, the day the whole 4th Armored crossed this German myth.

The German artillery response was dazzling and deafening,

but it was everything but deadly. Their stations were too far away; they illuminated the night with an incessant hail of translucent bombardment, but they drew no blood. Not that I was anxious to see German artillery draw blood, but there was something anticlimactic about the safety, and comparative ease, with which we forded this river. The fact that it was forded so easily is a tribute to the tactical and strategic genius of George Patton. The Germans had loaded up their Rhine defense at Mainz; that's where we were supposed to be. How could we be crossing anywhere else? American artillery fire had been smashing away at Mainz for days now. Of course, we weren't scoring *too* much. We had to leave them enough to defend the spot, and we had to make it not *too* difficult for them to reinforce it. So we gave Mainz a migraine, but there was no decapitation . . . and they girded up their loins at Mainz, and stockpiled shells and .88's, and waited, and waited. I would later learn that they were so embarrassed, they were angry and would beef up some later resistance in hopes of extracting revenge.

In the long run, however, Patton had saved lives, lots of lives. His taste for glory, his love for the symbolism of the Rhine and the grandeur of winning it in a mighty struggle, was not so prepossessing that he would shed blood to exaggerate that glory. He was still as much of a competent general as he was a figment of his own mythical imagination; he saw a possible snare, he laid it, and he won—savoring, I trust, the redemption of American lives as the real glory.

But the little old lady from Pasadena was not to be cheated of his share of histrionics. Once on the other side of the Rhine Patton fell to his knees and clutched two large handfuls of German mud. "Thus William the Conqueror," he intoned, an oblique reference to Hastings, when William accidentally tripped but made it seem that he was intentionally falling to his knees to personally manhandle English soil. The Norman legions would thus not interpret their leader's fall as a bad omen. Yes, there was always something esoteric about Patton's showboating. But if those histrionics were abstruse, his exuberance was well deserved. He had fooled Germans and saved Americans.

His greatest moment, however, had been earlier, during the actual crossing. That he was the first to cross the Rhine was an enormous feather in his cap, not simply because he was the first but also because Montgomery, his archfoil, was supposed to have been. What publicity attended Monty's preparations! Churchill had even recorded a speech for English radio praising his commander—and, agony of agonies, that speech was actually broadcast, just hours after the Third Army bested their English counterparts.

So Patton was not going to let his triumph pass without some gesture to memorialize it. He had beaten Monty by one day, and in one of the great moments of World War II he symbolized his personal victory. Now, what do you do for such a moment? After all the anguish of Tripoli and Sicily, the slapping incident, the frustrating subordination to Bradley, the itching knowledge of your own immortality and the presentiment that that immortal substance might fall to fallow ground, what the hell do you do?

Gen. George S. Patton unzipped his fly and pissed into the Rhine river!!

Now, this is no mere legend circulated through Third Army ranks and exaggerated or distorted from one telling to the next. No, it is very much a matter of historical record. I might add that Patton was photographed during this grand gesture, and I have a photostat of that shot, which I will cherish till my death. I wish I knew where the original glossy is, I'd show it to you. . . . Of course, the newspapers failed to pick up on this moment, which was only to be expected. I mean, it's not exactly like raising the flag on Iwo Jima.

So our historic slice into the heartland of the enemy was accompanied by—forgive me—a tinkle of brass. By nightfall of March 24, the advance guard of the 4th Armored was already capturing a number of small towns on the east side of the Rhine. A remarkable fact, really, when you remember that the rear of the division was still crossing the river. No, we didn't stop for any ceremony; the whole twisting column of the 4th Armored merely continued to extend its deadly woof and warp. Our next destination was the Main River. We gobbled up German soil and then bridged it.

And Hitler had given us a fine opportunity to resume our classic double-columned posture, our full and mighty consolidation of military identity. This opportunity occurred on the banks of the Main, where the Germans had built as good an autobahn as any in Eruope. It could have been Pine Camp. There were no terrestial impediments; our speed accelerated ever more mightily. We drove into Saxony, our destination the town of Chemnitz.

March 28. An extraordinary day. We took thirty-five towns and eight thousand prisoners. That was the largest crop in any single twenty-four-hour period in 4th Armored history. And for every one hundred prisoners taken, what did we have to do? Not much more than fire off a couple of rounds. The bell was tolling for Nazism, and there were eight thousand soldiers, doubtless more in other parts of the world, who had no desire to be buried with it. You should have seen how happy they were after they were captured! No trouble, no sabotage—the last thing they wanted to do was escape! But whatever the attitude of the prisoners themselves, eight thousand of them in one day, signed, sealed, and delivered, is outlandish. So how am I not supposed to use superlatives when I write about my division? And for this day, March 28, 1945, make up a banner!

March 29. Earthquake, volcano, the harrowing of hell. We rolled over German earth and reached the towns of Lauterbach and Grossenlüder. The earth split. Two enormous underground ammunition depots detonated, rending the ground above—twin geysers of pure fire, quick horrific fountains. Hundreds of 4th Armored men could have died; fortunately, the explosions were distant, and I doubt that anyone was hurt. But mark down March 29, 1945, as the day on which the underworld blew up.

March 30. We approached the town of Hersfeld. A bit of news came over the wire. President Roosevelt had given the 4th Armored Division a Distinguished Unit Citation. Now, there are two possibilities here. The first is that FDR never actually heard of us, and it was only during a conversation with Eisenhower that he was prompted to award the 4th Armored—and who knows, maybe Ike had needed prompting from Patton. But it is more likely—and certainly more worthy of a great war leader such as Roosevelt—that he was a man who truly appreciated his "butchers." After all, FDR was an aristocrat, and aristocrats eat meat. He could get the tenderizer from someone else, but we were his Chicago.

March 31, and April, and beyond. More would burn. At Kreuzberg the 35th Battalion encountered the German version of the scorched earth policy, something which the Wehrmacht did not need to bring home from Russia with them—for destroying your own land rather than letting the enemy have it is something that comes naturally to all peoples everywhere. The Russians have merely had the opportunities to use it more often—but the Germans did manage to demonstrate their prowess. Kreuzberg was rubble and stone. Bits of grass had already begun to sprout between broken cobblestones. It seemed like an ancient ruin—except, perhaps, for an occasional wisp of smoke lulling around a pile of barely smoldering rubbish.

There are many ways to scorch your own earth. The czar and Stalin and the Wehrmacht merely burned it; the SS was more expansive. A sizable detachment knifed their way through our lines and captured an American hospital at Attenstadt. This hospital was also serving as a center for

Allied movement and prisoner transport. Well, the SS captured a number of valuable Americans, including Harold Cohen, who would later tell the tale. The Nazi commander treated Cohen and the others with legal consideration but ordered all the German soldiers found at Attenstadt into the back of a truck. There, in punishment for having surrendered, they were machine-gunned, all of them. Then American infantrymen began to move in, and the SS withdrew, leaving their prisoners behind.

Cohen was sick. As soon as our infantry arrived, he organized a patrol and went looking for the beast who had ordered his own countrymen slaughtered. They caught up to his jeep, which had been blown from under him by American artillery. Pieces of his body were scattered nearby. So Cohen returned to the war.

Remember those medics in Brittany? It was the SS then who had stripped war of any dignity it might retain, and it was the SS who had now done the same. In a sense, though, these atrocities redound to the glory of humanity. There is no society so totalitarian that all differentiation is erased. Diversity triumphs as long as human beings are involved—for even within Hitler's military machine there were differences, vital differences. I never saw any member of the Wehrmacht commit an act of unnecessary brutality; if they did, those acts were the exceptions that prove the rule. The regular German dogface was fighting for Hitler; he was murdered by Hitler, but he did not succumb to the full brutality of Hitler's visionary perversion.

By early April we were taking camouflaged panzers by the dozen; many of these had been abandoned, others put up light resistance and then surrendered. A whole company of German tanks decorated with leaves and branches and two small airfields hidden in the brush guarded the outskirts of Gotha. These panzers gave us the toughest resistance we had seen in weeks, though they seemed too tired to charge, or perhaps they preferred to stay as close to the airfields as possible. In any case, it was a desperate defense; their fire was almost hysterical, as if they must have known that we'd eventually run them over. Bob Saville fought like a crazy man, perhaps because a medic had given him a tab of benzedrine to rid him of a diuretic complaint. His tank moved toward the airfields like a roadrunner; his fire was incessant. We took Gotha, Bob calmed down (but not before he vainly demanded a Congressional Medal), and we set our sights for the town of Ohrdruf.

We took it without significant incident, though a heavy German artillery barrage slowed our progress. A neat line of dead German infantrymen pointed the way from the outskirts to the center of the town. It was like following a row of tombstones to some dark destination—and little did we foresee how appropriate those signposts would prove or how dark that destination would turn out to be!

That darkness would not be immediately apparent, for our first taste of Ohrduf was one of dazzling fascination; the Germans had set up a labyrinthine underground communications network there preparatory to the now inevitable flight from Berlin. Radios, food supplies, cots, guns, ammunition, books, documents, even an old Victrola—exploring and appropriating it was fun, like going through somebody's attic. How many such networks survived, I wonder? How many Martin Bormanns made their way to South America via just such an otherworldly construction as the one we found at Ohrdruf?

We emerged from this subterranean cavern into a sunlight that would prove darker than any merely physical submersion. Three or four days we would spend at Ohrdruf, consolidating our line and assimilating reinforcements. And before we left the town, the 4th Armored Division would be the first American unit to liberate a concentration camp.

Most of the survivors had taken to the woods just before the Germans evacuated, for the Germans had sprayed the camp with gunfire as a last parting gesture. These survivors inched their way back toward Ohrdruf as they watched the Nazis flee. Most of them were still inching and crawling and wheezing when we found them. Ninety percent would die shortly after our arrival.

The cells and barracks themselves were another story. Most of the inmates were dead when we got there. A few were still alive, supine on their feculent straw mats or twisted around themselves on the dank floor. The building itself looked like a busted-out factory stinking amid high-growing weeds in one of America's uglier heartlands. We entered a stench of urine and vomit, and of decomposition—that ungodly mixture of feces and sulfur, hellfire in a sewer.

The Nazis had made an effort to disguise their barbarism by sprinkling chemicals on the corpses. To no avail. The gaping wounds, the festering sores and abrasions inflicted, no doubt, by a yawning soldier's casual gun butt, were clearly visible beneath the now granulated coagulations of lime. The survivors managed to lift up their heads in some effort to communicate. But they could only gurgle incoherently, and then their heads fell back down. In many instances they died there on the spot. Perhaps the shock of an American entry broke the thin skein between breath and blessed extinction.

And you know something? There were no gas chambers here, no ovens. Oh no, this was a small concentration camp, a distant outpost where inmates who weren't good enough for Buchenwald were kept. What makes it all the more horrible is that this unspeakable misery was but a prolegomena to ever-deepening circles of hell. If we could have seen this a year earlier, I guarantee you the war would have ended a year earlier. We would have galloped to Berlin. They could have shot our heads off, shelled our torsos, but somehow we would have kept moving or crawling—rolling armless and legless, if necessary, goddammit!—all the way to Berlin, until each of us, Jew and redneck, WASP and wop, could have laid some of our own restive flesh on the sallow, diseased carcass of Heinrich Himmler.

One memory, briefly related: There was a dead little boy, about six or seven, whose rectum had been shattered.

And then Patton came. Those who saw him said his face was tense with anger, but he wasn't raging. He had known of these camps, and now that he had found one, he would stay cool and carry out a little plan—perhaps his own, perhaps one that had been suggested to him. At any rate, that plan would be adopted elsewhere, in every town that housed a concentration camp. He personally escorted thirty citizens of Ohrdruf to the camp. Most of them looked away in disgust, while some of them no doubt silently cursed Patton for the tastelessness he had shown in bringing them there—but Old Blood and Guts knew the difference between war and murder. Think what you want about this man, his brand of glory in war was the precise antithesis of the incalculably sophisticated mechanism that could so efficiently eradicate six million civilians. Perhaps somewhere within him Patton *was* raging.

And the citizens with him shirked all moral responsibility. It was here at Ohrdruf that the shameful refrain began: "We didn't know. How could we know? This has nothing to do with us!" Well, they knew. Of course they knew—and probably they could also guess that this camp was but a scale model for dozens of others. Yet two of Patton's guests not only knew but submitted the most drastic possible testimony to that effect. This was the mayor of Ohrdruf and his wife.

I imagine the two of them stealing furtive glances at each other during the tour. What have we stood for? they're asking each other with their eyes. Well, they stood for nothing, and that was the problem. The man merely stood for the honor entailed in being mayor of a provincial town, while the woman merely stood for the status of being that man's wife. Nothing more. But whatever we stood for, those eyes say to each other, surely we must have stood against this—or did we? How could we? If we had, wouldn't we be dead now? No, we must have been for it, and how can we now separate ourselves from it, from all that it stands for, and from what it says about us? What kind of statement can we make?

I imagine the two of them returning to their home, neither speaking. Inside their living room, which now seems to be shrinking around them, an hour or two of silence passes. Then one of them mentions something of trivial, everyday interest. The other tries to respond. But what can we do now? What kind of statement can we make?

I imagine the woman falling asleep. When she awakens, she calls feebly for the mayor. No response. She rolls out of bed, grimacing in pain—some new pain, the source of which she had almost allowed herself to forget for a moment. She walks into the living room and sees her husband hanging from a beam. *So that was what you could do. That was your statement.* She feels obliged to be shocked, but she isn't. She goes into the kitchen, gets herself some rope. For her statement.

And at the very last moment. Grace. She ties the rope to the same beam and rejoins the man. Once again life has meaning; life has been renewed.

The two of them hanging together, side by side, a peaceful expression on their twisted faces: That I don't have to imagine. That's a matter of record. A matter of history.

And somewhere, perhaps at that very moment, in Berlin or Munich, a party of SS officers is listening to the glorious strands of Beethoven's Ninth. Such is Beethoven's shame. You can't hear him roar or grieve in his grave, for the sound of shells and tanks bursting all over Germany is deafening. Maybe you can't even hear his music. Maybe you can only see his ghost turning profoundly away from his homeland.

Then maybe no shame at all; such anger at human monstrousness doesn't need the accompaniment of any guilty sense of personal implication in a collective disgrace. What disgrace to him if SS officers paw his flowers with their sweaty, chancrous hands? And wasn't it Goering who said, "Every time I hear the word *culture*, I go for my gun"?

I went for mine as we pulled out of Ohrdruf.

We fought a fierce, bloody fight at Jena. I saw young men blown out of turrets, mutilated infantrymen, retreats and fears and surges of victory. It all seemed so noble after Ohrdruf, even the mutilations—for these were mutilations rendered by fields of force as they moved toward an objective as necessary as the sunrise. This was not "rational" science experimenting toward a great new future and sprinkling the monkeys with lime afterward. This was war, a rotten, miserable thing but hardly an unredeemable one. However you define glory, it was there, somewhere.

# 9
# The Extensions
# of Man

Once upon a time thirty American infantrymen were mowed
down by a nest of German machine guns. It was striking, how
vulnerable they were. How could they bear to wake up in the
morning knowing that they were protected by nothing more
than their own wits and the empty air around them? Well,
we're dealing with a wholly different way of looking at things.
Ask them what they think of the tanks and the men who drive
them. Ask them if they'd like to trade places. Most will keep
the evils they have, and run from the ones they know not. Nat
Frankel, on the other hand, will stay in his tank. You're not
cutting off my balls and sinking me knee deep in mud, and in
full view of a German gun! Keep things the way they are and
everybody's happy.

The infantrymen used to call the tanks steel coffins. No
statistic could ever dissuade them. I remember talking to a
wounded infantryman who was waiting for a light tank to pick
him up and take him to the hospital. He had taken a glancing
shot in the stomach—nothing exorbitant—and a deeper slug in
the thigh.

"You still think it's better outside?" I asked him, in

reference to a remark I had heard him make about what lunatics tankers have to be.

"I don't give a shit if you double the lead," he answered from his stretcher. "Just give me oxygen and I'll die happy."

Well, I think the time has come to outline and describe explicitly the machinery that circumscribed our lives from Normandy to Prague. Certain general but extremely important facts have already come to your attention—the fact, for example, that the tanks were so much an extension of us that our manhood, the very texture of our cocks and balls, was tied in with them. Let's fill in some of the spaces so that not only the civilian but the bemused and terrified infantryman as well can comprehend that manhood a little more clearly.

There were three kinds of tanks: lights, mediums, and heavies. The lights were used mainly for transportation of the wounded, for supply convoys, and for quick evacuations of one sort or another. The advantage of a light tank is, of course, its speed; it can elude enemy fire and escape the very presence of danger. The disadvantage lies in its vulnerability; if the light tank is hit, if circumstance or stupidity squeezes it into a hole from which there is no escape, it doesn't have a chance. The German antitank guns—which were .88s and tough on *all* American machinery—scored our lights by the dozen.

The mediums and the heavies were closer in style and impact to each other. Yet the heaviest of our heavies were not as lumbering, as thick-skinned, as imposing as the German heavies. As I have previously noted, this made for an essential difference between the Germans and us in strategies and tactics. The Germans counted on their immobility, their pure dogged strength. The 4th Armored, and others like it, relied on speed. The 4th Armored, and others like it, won.

Now, light tanks were not the only medium of American transportation. There were, of course, the half-tracks, constructed as their name suggests. Instead of having full treading, they had two wheels in front and a treading in back.

The top was open, and the material of the body was sheer tanklike steel. They weighed about eighteen thousand pounds and could make forty-five miles an hour; they usually carried three-inch machine guns. Faster than the medium tanks but tougher than the lights, the half-tracks were a blessing.

As effective as the half-tracks, however, were the brutal M32 six-by-six trucks. These mothers could carry a whole arsenal. Six-by-six means that there were six wheels, all of which were powered. The only thing I didn't like about them was the position of the Browning machine gun, which was on top of the front. It was really more exposed than the turret of a tank; firing one in combat was like sitting atop the Empire State Building and swatting jets. Even King Kong couldn't make that.

Fastest of all, of course, was the jeep—brand name Willys— the fastest transport of all at fifty-five miles an hour. And don't think they only transported officers. These jeeps were highly effective in moving supplies of various sorts. Good in a pinch for bullets, medicine, anything smaller than the trunk of a car.

All questions of tactical effectiveness notwithstanding, the panzers were the most fascinating tanks ever constructed. We've seen the Tiger 6s before; remember the officer with the handkerchief? But they were dinosaurs, eventually too big and dumb to succeed. They held six men instead of the customary five (all medium and heavy American tanks housed five), and sloshed through the mud of Singling like primeval beasts laboring vainly in the muck of the La Brea tar pits. Yet the sight of one was as riveting to me as the sight of a dinosaur would be to a small child.

If the Tiger 6 was a tyrannosaurus, the Sturmgeschutz 75 was an interminable viper slinking across the terrain. At twenty-two tons, it was the most mobile of German tanks and had a driving range of one hundred miles (the American range averaged around twenty miles less). But it made a hell of a nice target. Just fire low and you'd hit something, a fact that notably decreased its effectiveness. Fascinating to look at, but you don't win a war by fascinating the enemy.

There were four important guns affixed to American tanks. In the turret was the main man: the .76, a stationary phallus with which you could bust a tank or render a foot soldier unrecognizable. It is a tribute to the fighting skills of the 4th Armored that we were never sufficiently equipped with .76s until the run to Bastogne. Up till then we had been using the .75, which was like a peashooter in comparison. Had we had more .76s earlier, who knows how much faster we would have embraced Brittany and Alsace-Lorrain?

Besides the .76 we had a .50-caliber antiaircraft gun, a manual .30-caliber that was called the coaxial, and just next to the driver a bow gun. The latter moved in a forty-five-degree angle and was thus indispensable. If the machine itself could not maneuver to confront a danger on our parallel, the bow gun could—as effectively to the right as to the left.

There were two types of shells, both of which were necessary in winning World War II. The first was the armor-piercing, which functioned in precisely the manner of its name. It could tear through anything. Of course, you had to be close enough to use it; from too far away the only thing this shell would pierce was flesh. So at a certain distance the high-explosive shell was utilized; as it turned out, it was eventually more useful. Obviously, in close combat the high explosive would be as dangerous to your own ranks as to the enemy's. But to a division that barely halted from beginning to end, the decimation of a distant foe proved to be the more valuable premium.

The Germans had the bigger weapons, but ours worked faster. Yet a little more information will suffice to explain why our infantry preferred feet to treading. A tank, you see, had four gas inlets, and each one was filled with high octane. If any one of those four were hit, the whole machine could go up. The best you could hope for in the event of a hit was that only the treading would be scored. This would immobilize your machine, but you could stay inside (and hope that the Germans would uncharacteristically relent in their fire), or you could jump out and run for cover of some sort.

But when that gas got hit, your options were, to say the least, limited. Oh, we had a fire extinguisher, but that was for overheated motors; it was useless for an exploded tank. Now, there were two ways to get out: One was via the turret; the other was through a trapdoor on the opposite side of the driver from the bow gun. Often the turret would be inaccessible to anyone inside the tank; if the machine was hit badly, particularly if it was knocked on its side, the trapdoor would jam as well. At best you would have ninety seconds to get out that door; if it jammed, you would need fifty of those seconds to push it open. That would leave forty seconds for three men to squeeze out. Tick, tick, tick, boom!

And what would happen if both the turret and the trapdoor were inoperative? What would happen is, you'd die! It takes twenty minutes for a medium tank to incinerate; and the flames burn slowly, so figure it takes ten minutes for a hearty man within to perish. You wouldn't even be able to struggle, for chances are, both exits would be sheeted with flame and smoke. You would sit, read *Good Housekeeping*, and die like a dog. Steel coffins indeed!

But they were *my* steel coffins, and I loved them!

I suppose the Germans had it worse. Toward the end of the war, with the Saar in Allied hands, there was a disastrous shortage of oil. Imagine those enormous panzers, laborious at best, now having to rely on coal and wood for the least bit of movement. That rendered them all the more primitive: the fetid odor of burning wet lumber, the ejaculations of dark smoke—all in order to push a gigantic steel idol forward, inch by excruciating inch.

The more primitive those traps became, the more certain was their doom. At times it was almost sad. I remember an odd incident. We had just left Koblenz. Alongside the road was a smoldering Tiger 6, apparently the victim of American artillery. I saw Bob Saville inspecting it, so I jumped from my own machine to say hello. Inside the panzer was a little bundle of logs and a dead German. His clothes had been shorn right off by fire, but his face was relatively whole. His body was propped up against the side; Bob nudged him down, and when he fell, his penis shriveled, dropped to the floor, and landed in miniscule fragments of foreskin. Ouch!

Oh, and one more thing. You know, it's goddamn hard to get a good night's sleep in a tank.

The extensions of man. Something that does human work but exists outside the human body. A stick. An air conditioner. A gun. Technology. One thing I don't buy is the argument that guns don't kill people, people kill people. So what? A gun is an extension of man—and there are certain extensions that men must not make. There are certain reflexes in space, human movements in certain directions and dimensions, that must be limited. I'm not submitting an argument for gun control, but the National Rifle Association ought to get itself a more intelligent slogan.

So consider the tank. Consider it as an extension of man. What does it tell us about man? What fundamental fact of human nature does it manifest, what dark recesses of our beings does it hurl so ruthlessly into the light? The warriors of our era, our relentlessly efficient era, were not going to leave one stone unturned in devising a machine to fling man's unthinkable nature in man's own face. Around 1914 the age began when man resolved to make it impossible for himself to avoid the Medusa's head of his own soul.

The tank. It is ceaseless destruction, unstoppable except by another, even more infernal machine. It protrudes shafts of cold metal with which to fuck a landscape and, by fucking, raze it. But it's not big enough inside, no, not big enough inside to afford the humanity it contains room enough for rest and sleep and peace.

And after the tank came Hiroshima and the bomb—a cock so huge we can't even use it. I'm an old man, but sometimes I feel like the last stud left on the face of the earth.

# 10
# Bauming Out

The scene is a cabin in a German transport boat somewhere in the Mediterranean. A number of prisoners, American and British, drift through the hours in lassitude, remembering the past and their recent capture and anticipating, or trying to, the ambiguous future. One of these prisoners is a high-ranking American officer, past the first boundary of middle age; his face is that pure nondescript American military face, bland but stalwart. His eyes are clear, his mouth and cheekbones expressionless.

He gazes out at the blue, blue waters, and his thoughts are particularly tortured. What a future he had planned for himself! The Pentagon bureaucracy was a carte blanche credit card; he had all he needed to navigate every corridor, attain promotion to endlessly higher niches, mount every ridge—and toward what? Toward anything and everything! The Joint Chiefs of Staff! Who knows? But now this! What a slap in his face! The war wouldn't go on forever, but who knows what losses of opportunity, what taciturn ostracism of his professional possibilities, this synapse might present? He could wind up in some PW camp for years, and when he returns, someone else will have plucked all the plums his mouth had watered for.

His name is Waters, John Waters. He was captured in North Africa, where he had hoped to exploit the waning of Rommel's star to the fullest. But one day his outfit was encircled, and when he stepped out into the glaring sun, his boots worn gray by the steaming sand, a German soldier met him with the barrel of a German gun. Then, endless days waiting for assignment, the confusing transportation to a German port, and now the Mediterranean.

There isn't as much of German Europe as there had been when Waters first landed in Africa. There are only so many German PW camps left. The one his new masters pick for him is well to the east of the Rhine, in a dark green valley by the town of Hammelburg.

On March 26, 1945, Task Force Baum was organized and named after its leader—Abe Baum of the Bronx; at the time a captain, he would leave the service a major. His special unit consisted of Company A of the 10th Armored Infantry and two units from Baum's own 4th Armored: Company C of the 37th Tank Battalion, and one unit of light tanks from Company D of the 37th. All told, Task Force Baum was 293 men and 53 vehicles.

Baum's assignment was to strike northeast from where the main body of the 4th Armored units was located. Destination: the PW camp at Hammelburg. Objective: to liberate the fifteen hundred Americans imprisoned there. And there was another, ostensible—I repeat, ostensible—strategic purpose: to convince the Germans that the raid on Hammelburg was the vanguard of an enormous Third Army push. Of course, one German pilot with a pair of binoculars, flying in casual reconnaissance, would have been enough to debunk *that* illusion.

The order received on the twenty-sixth would brook no delay. Start immediately. Not tomorrow, nor the twenty-eighth, nor the twenty-ninth. Immediately. Hammelburg was sixty miles away, sixty miles of pure German entrenchment— and sixty miles back! And when you return, Captain Baum, the order might have read, you will have a Distinguished Service Cross and four Purple Hearts. And you will be shipped home to the Grand Concourse so fast you won't know what hit you!

The officers commanding Task Force Baum came from everywhere. There was Baum from New York. There was Lt. William Weaver from San Antonio, and Lt. Norman Hoffner from New Jersey, and Lt. William Nutto from Detroit. The fact that Task Force Baum was so geographically heterogeneous was no doubt accidental; I've never known the army to allot assignments on the basis of hometowns. But there was a grim appropriateness to the variety. Task Force Baum was the darkest of American missions, and, as such, required as broad a cross-section of Americana as possible.

The first action of the Hammelburg episode belongs, not to Task Force Baum, but to other units of the 4th Armored whose goal would be to clear a breakout path for the detachment. The village of Schweinheim was selected. We would have to clear the main street of all enemy deployment and free the town of snipers. Advance information had it that resistance at Schweinheim would be light, for the town was not highly valued by the enemy and whatever concentrations of men and weapons that had assembled there would quickly disperse to retrench elsewhere.

But it didn't happen that way.

Schweinheim was an inferno of German bazooka fire, ceaseless and pervasive. Our artillery was shelling all hell out of the area to the immediate east of the town, which was both good and bad. It was good for the obvious reason that it broke German resistance *there.* On the other hand, it gave the enemy in Schweinheim itself that much less reason for withdrawing. Why run from a tough fight to certain slaughter. No, the bazookas stood their ground and cauterized ours. It was less than three hours after Schweinheim was finally cleared that the men of the 4th gave it a sobriquet that has proved to be enduring: Bazooka City! Nobody remembers Schweinheim. But ask the right man about Bazooka City, and he'll quote you chapter and verse.

Within one hundred yards of the first building, a panzer-faust (German bazooka) pulverized an American tank. The men scrambled out and ran backward to safety; all save one made it. But the streets of Bazooka City were narrow, so narrow as to augment the already internecine power of the enemy fire. The damaged tank blocked all further progress. Fortunately, the flames subsided, and a soldier was able to sneak his way in with hopes that the machine was still drivable. It was, and he backed it up and out, allowing a second American tank to drive through. This tank was more successful; it attained the end of the street and sprayed the buildings on its left and right.

But the tank just behind it was creamed. This time we couldn't recover. German soldiers encircled it and started pummeling our infantry on both sides of the halted machine. As if that weren't hell enough, a couple of smart-ass Germans were cute enough to mount the tank, and take control of the still usable .76. For the first time in my knowledge of the 4th Armored an American gun was trained on American soldiers, and trained well! Our infantry countered and was thrown back. We tried again. The building closest to the American charge ignited completely; it looked like something out of the Chicago fire. The smoke and the heat were intense. Some of us couldn't see for the sweat, and the crackled reddening of our brows.

Then the radio blipped, and an unclear, worried, but somehow merciful voice ordered us to withdraw. It seemed we were beat, but victory can come in odd packages. We had already done heavy damage—at least thirty-five prisoners, and an indeterminate number of German dead and wounded. And as we withdrew, we blasted our front, and leveled the alcoves and rooftops where the Germans had stationed their bazookas. Enemy soldiers were hastening away in the distance, and by the time we had retreated back to the outskirts of Bazooka City, the town was somehow clear! We were lucky bastards. Or were we? Had we not cleared the town, Task Force Baum might never have been sent. Perhaps we would have radioed in a message of defeat, and an order might have come an hour or so later, saying, Forget the whole goddamn thing. Everyone would have been better off, and I mean everyone!

Such, however, was not the hand fate would deal. Task Force Baum drove unmolested down the main street of Bazooka City—but unmolested only in the sense that a gun fighter is unmolested during the two or three minutes he takes to get within range of a deadly adversary. They disappeared into the distance, into the dark. A trapdoor was closed behind them. They were gone, and each member of the detachment must have sensed the irrevocable isolation, the almost lunatic finality with which physical proximity to the main body of the 4th Armored Divison was severed.

No one tried to pretend that they understood why this was happening. Hammelburg? Fifteen hundred relatively well-treated American prisoners? And an almost impossible set of odds for three hundred seasoned and valuable warriors? It couldn't possibly be worth it! And a strategic bluff? Throwing away three hundred Americans for a dubious bluff when victory was now inevitable anyway? No, something else had to be happening somewhere, something of which Abe Baum himself, not to mention Nat Frankel, could hardly be aware.

Even a messenger could not get through—and if he could have, so what? There was no Seventh Cavalry out there to charge in and chase away the iron-helmeted Apaches. All Baum could do was utilize and rely on the 4th Armored's invariable weapon—its speed. And that is what he did. He ran his detachment like a racehorse to Gemünden, halfway to Hammelburg. Then Rieneck. Then Grafendorf. Then nothing.

Radio contact was lost. No one knew where he was, or if he was. In the meantime, the 4th Armored had to go about its business. We crossed the Main at Hanau, which is not to be confused with the capitol of North Vietnam. I can see, however, how the confusion could happen. Hammelburg was a foretaste of Hanoi, and An Loc, and Da Nang. In many respects, more ignoble.

Ten days. He was still lost, and finally he was reported MIA. Baum and the men with him were written off and replaced. Then on April 9, 1945, thirty-five men crawled back to our divisional lines to tell their horrible tale. They described how Baum had been captured and placed in a hospital, which had, however, been liberated three days earlier. Abed now in an American hospital, Baum himself would punctuate the narrations of the thirty-five survivors. He would tell how his task force had captured an enemy general and his staff, how they had blown out trains, tanks, towns, and men. How half of Task Force Baum was dead before they got to Hammelburg. And how the mission failed. How they rescued the prisoners but were trapped and blown away coming home. How they left their wounded lying in the road in hopes that the Germans would find them and save their lives. How there had been no other choice.

I am not writing this narrative in a straightforward style because it wasn't a straightforward event. The power elite has shrouded it in mist—that mist so merciful to men who often find it necessary to obscure the fact that they err and sin, shamelessly, incompetently. History saw it happen, let it pass, and lacked comprehension—and so did I. History got a few more details and went back over it—and so did I. Then history got the last of the truth and went back over it again—and so will I. No, there was nothing straightforward about the way in which Hammelburg, like Vietnam, evolved its way into the twisted, columnar yarn of American history. So let's go back over it again, this time relying on Abe Baum, a man of truth as well as courage, for a description of more and more of the devils contained in Pandora's box. And finally I'll give you the climactic fact of the matter as history would finally give it, a fact so monumental in its implication of moral paltriness that Baum would have opted for the stockade before charging into battle—had he only known it at the time!

No, they didn't even stop to eat after Bazooka City closed up behind them. They encountered heavy fire at Haibach and at Grunmorsbach, machine guns and bazookas and artillery. Men died, but no machines were lost. Good enough. On such a mission as this, the machines were worth more because without them no one would make it. Count your odds. Calculate what you've got, what you must expect to lose, and what you simply cannot lose. Let half your men die, but protect those tanks so that the other half of the human presence might make it. Play your percentages.

At night the inadvisability of even the quickest stop was more insistently felt. Task Force Baum never ceased firing; even when no enemy troops were visible, they fired. Whatever moved in a distant brush, whatever shadow seemed out of place, whatever had the least taint of suspiciousness, was shot at. They came upon Aschaffenburg, a heavily fortified town. Like nomadic bandits, they sneaked around and past it. Had they adventured the city, Task Force Baum would have been short-lived indeed!

But they were more vulnerable soon after, suffering continuous losses to Rechtenbach: a soldier here, a jeep there. Lohr, finally, and a great victory for Task Force Baum. Though one American tank was completely demolished—and each individual tank was a vital organ to the detachment—a column of charging panzers was obliterated. Twelve of them, totalled! It was a coup worthy of the 4th Armored in full regalia, but here a handful of virtual kamikazes in red, white, and blue did the trick. Eleven panzers bogged down behind their lead, who had been hit badly. The Americans meanwhile got a bead on the rear of the column and trapped them all. The fire raged for a good hour until there was nothing left but the smoking carcasses of the Tiger 6s, strewn around Lohr like carrion in the Sahara.

More triumph from Lohr to Gemünden. Task Force Baum sighted enormous brigades of German trains and secured firing angles from which the hapless enemy transports could find no sanctuary. All told, the Americans devastated 250 boxcars, wasting antiaircraft guns, pillboxes, soldiers, ammunition crates. Whatever else can be said about the Hammelburg mission, this much is incontrovertible: They did their damage! The more damage they wreaked, however, the more conspicuous they grew, and the more resolved became the enemy to swat this plague of a pest. That resolution was nearly satisfied at Gemünden.

It is unlikely that the Germans intended to finish off Task Force Baum at Gemünden. Their tactic was probably to deal a sizzling blow to the American gut and thereby decrease their chances of survival later on. If that was their goal, Gemünden was a German job well done. Bazooka concentration was the heaviest since Schweinheim; three American tanks were incapacitated. And worse yet—the enemy completely destroyed a vital bridge across the Saale just as Task Force Baum was preparing to use it. Fortunately, there were no tanks and only two men on it at the time; those two men were catapulted upward by the explosion and they somersaulted in midair. When they finally came down and splashed in the now impassable waters, their humanity was barely perceptible.

A whole German division had been at Gemünden, and another wasn't far off. More than likely, the Germans were a bit confused. I doubt that they expected the whole Third Army to be coming through; their reconnaissance couldn't have been that bad! Yet they must have been totally bewildered by the presence of such a small task force pocketed between two of their freshest divisions. Well, of course they were confused, but their confusion was little boon to the lost Americans. After all, the Germans didn't need a lucid comprehension of the situation to simply blow all fuck out of three hundred enemy intruders, whatever the purpose of that intrusion!

In the meantime, Task Force Baum continued to score points, even after the setback at Gemünden. At Bergsinn they captured a German general and his staff; the captivity could not, of course, have lasted very long (to whom could they transfer the prisoners?), but just to detain an enemy officer of any power was a feather in their cap. Who knows what delays in troop deployment they might cause by deactivating a general for even a mere twenty-four hours? Who knows what administrative snafus they effected by their action, and who knows how many of their own men and machines they may have saved in the process?

This was certainly the time for Task Force Baum to do as much damage as possible, for none of them could know what opportunities they would have in the immediate future. Somewhere in the back of each of their minds they knew they were on a suicide mission; they didn't want to die, but they expected to, much more pointedly than they ever had before, and so they reacted accordingly. Abandonment yielded a certain relish. They weren't going to forget the PW camp that had inspired their mission, but that was still an abstraction. The twelve panzers at Lohr, the general at Bergsinn—they were concrete. Contrary to theological speculation, I can tell you, in fact, I can guarantee it, that men on the brink grab for what's palpable and real before them—not some hazy expectation of a hazy future. In other words, you've got twenty German balls at Hammelburg and ten at Bergsinn; stomp the ten, for you may never see the twenty.

At Grafendorf they came upon a handful of Germans guarding two hundred Russian prisoners. They shot some of the Germans; the others fled. Now, what do you do with two hundred Russians in the middle of an American suicide mission? Of course, there wasn't anything to do. They said, "Hello, how are you?"—and then they released them. The Russians were canny enough to scatter. Had they stayed in one pack, they would soon have been recaptured en masse. So they fled to the woods in groups of four and five, or ten at the most.

Two points here fascinate me. First of all, why would the Russians have wanted the Americans to release them? Their captors weren't going to kill them; in fact, by staying with the Germans, they were ensuring their lives and certainly putting some sort of food in their bellies. I don't think it was either courage or patriotism that made them welcome release and so jeopardize themselves all over again. It was, rather, something primal in human nature. To know you are nothing but a lump of flesh in the arms of your worst enemy is, despite whatever minimal creature comforts you enjoy, a horrible, wearying living death. Better to chance complete extinction in order to feel like a wild animal instead of a caged one! And yet I had seen Germans run, almost elatedly, into our capturing arms. But give those same Germans time, a little time; let them taste the dehumanizingly unleavened bread of a PW camp, and they'll welcome escape, too, happy now to risk the narrow ledge between our suspicious vigilance and the savage discipline of the SS.

And a second, smaller point fascinates me. Task Force Baum is a documented adventure whose labyrinths gain greater and greater illumination as time goes by. But what the hell happened to those Russians? Each one of their destinies from the moment they left their captors at Grafendorf would justify a book or a movie. And how many other lives in how many other similarly drastic situations all over the world were equally worthy of extensive narration? To repeat a point I've made before, war is an embarrassment of riches.

The town of Ober, a mile and a half from Hammelburg, was fired in every way; the artillery was particularly heavy. But no one died. The men of Task Force Baum blinked into the mammoth ignitions, they perspired, they tried to talk, they moved on. Two bridges were accessible and were crossed, hurriedly, nervously. They came upon Hammelburg itself, a sleepy nondescript sort of place; the prison camp was just beyond it.

Yet even now they would have to fight before attaining their goal. Between the town of Hammelburg and the camp itself was a hamlet—more like a railroad junction (echoes of Bastogne)—called Pfaffenhausen. Here Task Force Baum scored mightily. It wasn't so much the column of infantrymen they mowed down, nor even the three panzers they destroyed; what gave Pfaffenhausen all the trappings of a major American triumph was the sight of forty-six German ammunition trucks, no doubt earmarked for further fortification of the camp itself, blown from hell to breakfast. Imagine forty-six stacks of TNT going off within a radius of two miles—and all in a period no greater than thirty minutes! And if those trucks had managed to reach their destination, the camp would probably have been impregnable. In the long run it wouldn't have mattered much, for the actual capture of the camp would eventually prove useless. But at least they took it—yes, goddammit, they took it—which must be some sort of consolation to the survivors, if not to the dead.

The camp was built into a hollowed-out circle of terrain, like a muddied fruit bowl. The whole approach was thus an incline, a natural and formidable trench. German infantrymen stationed themselves and their machine guns on the sloping side closest to the camp, giving them a somewhat obscure view of the charging Americans—but not so obscure that the heads of the men in their turrets weren't sighted. Most of the men who died taking the camp died with bullet holes in their foreheads.

The camp was in Baum's hands in two and a half hard hours. Once Baum's .76s had swept the hillock clear of Germans, there was barbed wire to smash, and every small delay in clearing or ripping the wire proved to be a deadly opportunity for German artillery and bazookas. Just beyond the barbed wire were pillboxes. They must have dug them in while the task force was battling at Pfaffenhausen. They had apparently seen no need to hurry. They figured that every bit of damage done to the Americans before the actual fight at the camp would just up the ante that much more crucially. And they had the aces.

Past the barbed wire was the stockade, parallel to the pillboxes, off to the side a few hundred yards. A naturally protected edifice, it afforded the Germans a brutally tough blockhouse from which to pummel the invaders. But Baum and his men were either going to win or die. How could they turn back? Back to what? The return to Allied lines would be tough enough; why bother even trying to survive without first completing the mission? So twenty .76s were trained on the stockade, and they maintained an incessant fire while the rest of the detachment concentrated their guns wherever a German soldier or weapon was visible.

There were small but billowing lines of falling men, dying Americans. The medics were racing everywhere until Baum, or one of his subordinates, got smart. Fifteen or twenty of the enemy had been captured between the sloping approach to the camp and the inner circle beyond the barbed wire; these Germans were forced to form a semicircle around the medics as they worked on the American wounded. It was a grand gesture, however futile (futile, for I doubt that any of the wounded attended by these medics would, in fact, survive)—and apparently there weren't enough SS men around to mow down the ring of Germans in order to kill the Americans within.

The stockade was silenced. The tanks grew ever nearer to the main building. In the distance German infantrymen were drawing back. All that was left was the guard detail: tough corporals and sergeants who whipped their men out of the relative safety of the barracks. Lugers and rifles in hand, they charged, fell back, stood their ground, and died. Hammelburg was liberated.

The PWs rushed out of the camp and embraced the men of Task Force Baum. Again, we see that primal rush of exhilaration that comes with the first taste of freedom, however dangerous or even fatal that freedom might be. Didn't they know they could all be killed trying to get back? Maybe they didn't know. Maybe they thought Patton was there, and Bradley just behind. In any case, they were a happy bunch of bastards. They jumped up on the tanks and grabbed whichever man they could—officer or dogface, it didn't matter. Hugged him, even kissed him. The whole camp looked like a schooner sitting in a Polynesian port.

Then, after the initial burst of euphoria subsided, the somber task fell to Baum and his officers to decide who was too sick to attempt the return home. Their responsibility was lightened by the obviousness of many cases. There were infections, badly tended wounds, malnutrition, and scurvy; there were a few men who couldn't control their water or their bowels—victims, not of German cruelty or neglect, but of the simple absence of necessary supplies and time.

So a few hundred remained to await the return of the German infantry while the rest set out west, toward the Third Army line; the odds against them weren't difficult to calculate. Nick the Greek would have put it at about a thousand to one. And Abe Baum knew it, if no one else did. But I tend to doubt that Abe's pessimism was based on information that was exactly exclusive. But what the hell, there was nothing else to do.

Oh, and there was one man who did *not* remain behind in Hammelburg camp. His name was John Waters.

Fifty yards out of Hammelburg a bazooka destroyed an American tank. Fifty yards, just fifty fucking yards! And where the hell did that bazooka come from? An evil portent, to be sure, as evil in its way as the undisturbed silence that ensued for what seemed the next thousand miles. Of course, the silence ended; it ended at a town called Hollrich. And Hollrich was only the beginning.

Three more American tanks were destroyed at Hollrich—three tanks, and a score of infantrymen. The Germans were going in for the kill; they had allowed the mouse to grab off the cheese, but the trap was a big one and could be sprung now, or fifty miles from now. There could be no question of a major American reinforcement; the enemy knew that Task Force Baum was naked. Slowly, methodically, the Germans began to take back the newly liberated prisoners.

Baum had some more heavy-duty thinking to do. He withdrew his detachment east, to a spot marked on his map as Hill 427. There he took stock and reorganized. But there wasn't much stock to take; the reorganization would not be particularly laborious. He had only a handful of tanks left, many of which were light. Those light tanks would come in handy if he could now manage to elude German fire of any sort; they would move faster and facilitate what had to be a speedy withdrawal. If they were hit, however, those three lights would go fast. And the men? Of the nearly three hundred who had set out from Bazooka City, one hundred and ten were left.

Then it happened. The Germans threw their heavy jab, the one they had been holding back and tensing and strengthening for days now. They encircled the hill and moved in—you've heard of Slaughterhouse 5? This was Slaughterhouse 427! German infantry poured through like rats heading for a carcass; artillery fire increased tenfold, blocking any kind of an effective American evasion. Task Force Baum had no choice but to sit and take it. The panzers rolled in, and Baum, though he was a seasoned warrior long before Hammelburg, would attest to the fact that he had never seen such rapid fire emerge from the turret of a German tank.

A mile away was a square, somber building. Immediately before the German attack, Baum had left dozens of wounded from Hollrich, and other weary men smarting from earlier wounds, within this shelter; he had scribbled a huge red cross on the facade. But German fire at Hill 427 spread in every direction; what the tanks weren't hitting, the distant artillery was. And then a direct hit, probably from the artillery, smashed the makeshift hospital. It exploded in half like faulted earth in a quake too large to measure. There was no Richter scale here in any case; the only indicator was the simple fact that no one within could have survived, or did survive.

What was Baum facing? Aside from the infantry, who poured in in a constant stream, the task force was surrounded by three columns of panzers—about twenty tanks to his seven. Men with dangling limbs and blown-out bellies continued to fire— but this was no heroic persistence. This was the sheer doggedness of the already dead. Dead, but not wanting to die, they had no choice but to caress their triggers with whatever lump of flesh they could manipulate. Oh, this legion of the undead did its damage, but still, still, they died too slowly, and with insufficient reason. They were dying too slowly for a cause distinguished not merely by their own courage but by the moral turpitude with which their superiors were testing that courage.

All American tanks were now inoperative. Our soldiers withdrew from their vehicles, including the jeeps and half-tracks, which were also burning. There was a brief hiatus, during which the men would normally have returned to their halted machines to see what they could salvage. But enemy concentration was too heavy. It would be certain death to check out anything. And what did that mean? It meant the greatest catastrophe and indignity in the history of the 4th Armored Division; it meant that Task Force Baum was now afoot! We—and I say "we," because they were part of us— were stripped of everything by which we had lived, the cold and metallic churches in which we had prayed and slept and murdered, everything by which we had so dynamically forged our own identity.

Afoot! The fight at Hill 427 had lasted a mere twenty-five minutes, but it was the fiercest German assault ever perpetrated against any unit of my division. Had they come across the 4th Armored itself, I doubt that they would have prevailed or even comported themselves as the 5th Para had done at the Bulge. But no matter; the savagery with which they wiped out Task Force Baum at Hill 427 was unparalleled. They fought and butchered so impressively—well, hell, they must have thought they were us!

Baum and his survivors took to the woods like wounded rogue bears. What ensued was horrific. The Germans fanned out from the POW camp, and from Hammelburg itself, with a score of bloodhounds. There is something so awful about that—whether in a war, a police chase, or a civil rights struggle in some Gothic backwoods. How else to be hunted down like a dog except by a dog? It brings the hunted down to the animal level. A man chases you, a man catches you—you yourself are still a man. But the dogs howled, sniffed the ground, and lusted, and the scents couldn't have been hard to pick up. Hollrich, Hill 427, the camp site itself were littered with fragments of blood-stained American clothes and pieces of American flesh. It was the strongest scent in the world.

Abe Baum was captured and taken to a POW hospital. I've never asked him, but I'm sure that he himself could not at that moment assess the extent of his wounds. He had been hit relatively early in the campaign and had made do with dirty strips of cloth to cover the numerous tears in his flesh. What a remarkable man! Not by nature a barbarian, he found himself in a barbaric situation, forced for weeks to strip away layers of his own hesitancy, the innate timidity contained in every man—and push on and on.

Luck would be with him now, however. The hospital to

which he was taken was run for the most part by captive Serbs. These medics and orderlies hid Baum and a number of others in recesses of their hospital; they obscured his identity and saw to it that he would not be reassigned to some other camp, deeper within the enemy heartland. By war's end, we would have to restrain many Serbs from wreaking unnecessary and savage revenge—however, by and large, these men who convenienced Baum typified the heroism of their people.

On April 6, the same day Baum was reported at Gotha to be missing in action, the hospital in which he lay was liberated by a wing of the American army. Hammelburg and the POW camp it hosted were still German, but Baum himself was reprieved and now could tell his tale. In the meantime, the thirty-five men who had been able—God knows how!—to escape the bloodhounds crawled back, themselves like chastened bloodhounds, to the American line. They told their tale as well.

I heard a cute story a few years later. Four men crawled out of the woods, into a clearing where six infantrymen were on patrol. It was immediately apparent that these beaten men could not be of any other party but Abe Baum's.

"You've come back," said one of the infantrymen.

The fugitive looked up, his face a welter of cuts and sweat. "Of course, I've come back," hissed this man who, all things considered, had no business being alive. "If I didn't come back, I wouldn't be here."

"No shit," answered the infantryman.

Cute, isn't it?

Now, I'm a bastard, I'm a real jokester. I've got that last fact of history for you, that last clod on the inside track down which history sometimes races to truth. But being a real jokester, I like to save the punch line for last, and after that I walk away with not much else to say. So here it is, the punch line:

*John Waters was George Patton's son-in-law!* Like everyone

else at the camp, he was liberated—and then recaptured. He'd have to sit out the rest of the war after all.

Maybe I do have a few more things to say. First of all, if you don't believe me, ask John Toland or Charles Whiting. They'll tell you all about the marriage that could have led Waters to the acme of Pentagon power; instead, it led three hundred men to an unnecessary grave. But don't ask Ladislas Farago. In an eight-hundred-page biography of Patton he doesn't see fit to mention Hammelburg, but he knew all about it. He had every relevant document that ever pertained to George Patton right there on his shelf.

So the warrior god was tarnished. How does all of this—this terrible, terrible bit of miscreance—square with the ambivalent but essentially admiring portrait of Patton I've painted heretofore? There are three ways of reacting: I could say, Forget it, fuck Patton, his fiasco at Hammelburg undermines everything he ever accomplished, gives the lie to his dreams of himself and his anachronistic devotion to glory. There was no glory here. Hammelburg didn't even have the redeeming glory of dynamic self-seeking. Instead, it was a petty, low effort, a selfish attempt to inject nepotism into war. But war doesn't lend itself to nepotism; politics does, not war. So what do we have here? We have George Patton, whose whole self-image relates profoundly to a stinging contempt for politics and the way it undercuts the nobler deeds of the soldier. And what does he do? He takes one of the most ignoble aspects of politics and, since it's to his own practical advantage, degrades his self-proclaimed vision of war with it. The shameful hypocrite! Forget every good thing I ever said about him!

But no, that's going much too far. George Patton is not the first man who failed to live up to himself. He erred tragically, he showed an underbelly of humanity that no moral philosophy can excuse. That does not mean, however, that the rest of him was a lie. Indeed, if you consider how shabby most human beings seem when standing before the eternal bar, one can only marvel at how steadfast he managed to remain—not merely to a principle—but to an impossible dream of grandeur that only a master of the High Renaissance could have consummated. And that on canvas, not on the dark and bloodied ground of a world war.

I'm not excusing Patton; I'm simply trying to salvage the rest of him, which was, I firmly believe, worth salvaging. How could I excuse him? He killed my friends (though Lord knows how many of us his genius rescued elsewhere), and for what? Consider this: Patton must have known that the chances of Task Force Baum actually liberating the camp and bringing Waters home were slim. So what was he doing? He was taking a wild swing, doing whatever he could for his son-in-law, which wasn't much, but something. "Yeah," he might have said, "there isn't much chance, maybe a thousand to one, but I can spare three hundred lives to take that chance. And if we make it, we make it. If we don't, only three hundred have died."

And consider this, too: Task Force Baum was almost Task Force Cohen. It was Harold Cohen who was first offered the job. But Cohen had more than a slight inkling that something was fishy. He knew damn well that the raid on Hammelburg could not have been conceived as a bluff to convince the Germans the Third Army was attacking behind. He knew that Patton himself could never have been so stupid as to contrive such a tactical blunder. Somebody was lying somewhere. And Cohen had too much status, and too many valuable hierarchical connections—so he was able to say, "Naw, I don't feel too well. I got a bellyache. Get someone else." They got Baum, whose inside information was more limited, as were his friends. But what do Cohen and Baum, the two men chosen to command this suicide mission, have in common? They were both Jews! "Yeah," Patton might have said, "if I'm going to throw away a valuable commander, make it a kike." At least

David had a more sanguine reason for arranging the death of Bathsheba's husband in combat.

Oh no, I'm not excusing George Patton.

But I want to understand his wretched mistake more thoroughly if only to preserve the texture of his real and great glory. There's a second way of reacting to Patton and Hammelburg. Like many great men, wasn't he also a tragic man? Wasn't he cursed, like a Greek hero, with a tragic flaw that brought him down and devastated the lives of those around him? A truly sympathetic way of reacting, but as badly chosen as any completely unmitigated rejection of his life and vision. A tragic flaw is rooted in the character himself, what he is and how he perceives. Patton's action at Hammelburg had little if anything to do with the lineaments of that character or those perceptions.

No, there's a third way of reacting, and, I believe, the truest one. Hammelburg was simply an abrogation of Patton's character; in short, *he wasn't himself* when he ordered the raid. Such self-forgetfulness is as dangerous as self-destruction directly commissioned by the dark recesses of the unconscious. Obviously. Look what happened. Patton stopped being Patton in order to rescue a relative, and three hundred men died. And then something else as well: Hammelburg was unquestionably one of the main reasons behind Patton's abrupt dismissal from command of the Third Army. Could there have been any other important reason? After the triumphs of the preceding year, could there have been one other single important reason?

But Patton is salvaged because what Patton did at Hammelburg had nothing to do with what he had been at Avranches, at Bastogne, crossing the Rhine. I think this lapse in him makes him all the more an appropriate symbol of the American military. Remember how popular the movie *Patton* was? It wasn't popular simply because it was brilliantly written and acted. That film showed us genuine American glory, a real sustenance right smack in the middle of the Vietnam War. Vietnam was the great American loss of self, a mighty, terrible destruction of all nobility. We turned to Patton then for a return to valor, for an image of ourselves and of our glory. We needed it then. But now we learn that Patton, too, had forgotten himself and lost his glory. Well, on behalf of an America that didn't know who it was at Da Nang, I'll remember Normandy and Gettysburg and Yorktown; on behalf of a Patton who was missing in action at Hammelburg, I'll remember Brittany, and the Bulge, and what is still ahead, the end of World War II and the triumph of American decency.

So let's finish Hammelburg off as quickly as we can; we've paid it our dues. The three dozen survivors, including Baum himself, were processed and shipped back to the States almost immediately, regardless of whether or not they were actually due to be released. Medals were handed out, personal commendations made floridly but inconspicuously. Yes, this handful of men were rewarded for their gallantry and bribed for their silence.

And how, after enunciating the dimensions of Patton's role, can we adequately sum up Abe Baum? "By his deeds," John Wood—whose presence would have prevented the whole brutal chapter—would have said, "and by his deeds alone shall you know him." Oh, by the way, Baum's done very well for himself. He lives now with his family in Rancho Palos Verdes, California. Having emerged from the service a major, he started his own company and named it the Major Blouse Company.

Pretty hokey, but what the hell!

There's nothing left now but to end the war. Let's not draw it out any more than we need to. But let us not forget that the end of a war is as precarious and as multifaceted as the first blistering rounds of fire on a hitherto silent plain. War begins in quiet and ends in hubbub, then quiet again; all that has intervened is a mere continent of corpses.

The 4th Armored was heading toward a rendezvous with the Red Army. Rendezvous with destiny—speaking of which, FDR died. We observed five minutes of silence, which was our only pause in a one-hundred-mile sweep. Forty miles away were the Russians, but it was not our eventual fate to make that linkup. It would fall to the First Army to consummate the supreme consolidation of the anti-Nazi legions. We turned west, then south on the Autobahn, toward Bayreuth, which we took.

Bayreuth. A big place for Hitler. Here it was that Wagner had conned King Ludwig II into bankrupting Bavaria in order to build a massive house for German—specifically Wagnerian —opera. Here it was that all the Germanic myths that swirled around in Hitler's head, lending a mad legitimacy to the slaughter and genocide, were enacted to the tunes of late Romantic decadence. Hitler himself could sit here for hours, sometimes days—and command others to do the same, through consecutive performances of the *Ring Cycle,* in tracts of time that seemed detached from time itself. It may well be that Bayreuth, not Berlin, was the great seat of Nazi power, though it was not a power of any directly military or political aspect.

If Beethoven turned over in his grave at the sight of Ohrdruf's citizens hiding away from the stench of a horror they themselves had allowed, Wagner's odd spirit was unsettled, not by any deeds of the SS (which he probably would have commended), but by the incredible vision of the 4th Armored Division frolicking in his gigantic opea house. We had a few days in the city, you see, and felt free to explore it. Somebody —God knows, I wish I knew his name—had organized the 4th Armored Follies, to be held on the big stage at Bayreuth. Yeththir! You don't want to miss it! Laughs galore! All the pretty ladies in the world! Hear Pvt. Joe Schtunkhead of Cleveland sing "Melancholy Baby," right here where Siegfried first kissed his little cutie, Brunnhilde!

Actually there were far too few females. Instead, we were treated to half the noncoms in the 4th Armored (myself definitely excluded) in drag, kicking up hairy legs and intoning "See What the Boys in the Back Room Will Have." And lecherous verses to "Lili Marlene." Then a Pvt. Curt Something-or-Other sang "Give My Regards to Broadway." Great cheer. And a comic of sorts, doing a Henny Youngman routine circa 1915. Take my wife, please. I played a club in Jersey, it was so tough the hatcheck girl's name was Dominick. Take my wife, please!

Wagner definitely turned over in his grave. Good for him.

And then back to work. We were to reassemble on the Danube, north of Deggendorf. On the way there I fell behind the rest of my 8th Battalion by some seventy-five yards—just pure laziness on my part. As I began to speed up, I felt something give beneath us. The treading had skipped, or something was wrong with the motor. We'd probably lose the 8th now, but at least we knew where we were going, we weren't under direct fire, and we would no doubt catch up in good time.

But I couldn't get the goddamn thing fixed. My bow gunner and I were working on it for what had to be a good half hour. We were absorbed in concentration, muttering suggestions to each other and simply not bothering to look up. It wasn't the first time I let my guard down; I had let it down in more precarious situations. This, however, would certainly be the last time I would take anything for granted.

Finally, it was fixed. I ordered the driver to test it, and he was able to push on ahead some twenty feet. I rose to join him. Then I heard it. "Halt!" I was a goddamn prisoner of war. Goebbels was ready to sing "The Star Spangled Banner," and I was a prisoner of war!

They ordered us to march to our left, which we did. Arriving in a secluded spot between three large boulders, we found a small German party, perhaps a patrol, perhaps stragglers. The highest-ranking German there was a captain, a tall man with slick strands of gray hair combed straight back. I gave him my name and rank. I still can't believe that anyone would actually give a shit about my serial number.

We sat there with them for a full hour. They must have been discussing their plan of action. My Yiddish isn't quite good enough to afford me immediate comprehension of German, but I'm almost positive that they simply didn't know in which direction to proceed. The captain and a subordinate stepped away for a few moments, perhaps to reconnoiter, which set the scene for a remarkable incident—and one that confirms previous thoughts of mine concerning the diversity extant even within the Nazi war machine.

While the captain was away, one of the German dogfaces grabbed my arm. At first I didn't know why, so I pulled it back, and, a bit precipitate, I waved my first threateningly across the periphery of his face. He struck me with the butt of his rifle, enough to stun me into a momentary unconsciousness. When I awoke, my watch had come off my wrist and onto his.

The captain returned, and I snarled out a complaint, really just to be nasty—because I was sure the watch was now ancient history. Lo and behold, the captain walks over to the thieving soldier and kicks him in the face. Then in the side. Out comes the luger—but he didn't point it, he held the tip upward, portentously. The soldier took off the watch and returned it. I could understand what the captain said next, for he said it slowly, effectively drawing out each syllable. "You are a disgrace," he said. "You are a disgrace to the Wehrmacht."

As indeed he was. Now that officer's long gray hair retains a symbolic meaning for me; I associate it with integrity, with honor, with something so stubbornly decent in human nature that even enlistment in a Hitlerian cause can't eliminate it. That captain knew he was beaten, maybe dead—but he wasn't going to lose what he had lived for and lived by just because destiny had outplayed him.

Yet I had always feared capture. What if there had been no venerable authority present? Indeed, as early as Normandy I had exploited an odd mistake. On each soldier's dog tags was one of three letters: either *C* for Catholic, *P* for Protestant, or *H* for Hebrew. I had been sent a *C* by mistake, and so another tag, with an *H*, had been requisitioned. But I knew whom I was fighting; I knew that Julius Streicher was no Talmudic scholar. I kept the *C* tag and always wore it into combat; the *H* I wore at less dangerous times. There had been, however, nothing dangerous about the drive to the Danube, so—wouldn't you know it?—I was wearing the *H* the one and only time I was captured. Lord knows, it might have mattered had I been in less distinguished company.

A sound of engines roared in on our right. The Germans had to move fast to their left; it was now the only direction open to them, and they didn't have the time to take us with them. They gathered their things and started to run. "Auf Wiedersehen," said the captain to me, the highest-ranking American present.

"God be with you," I said, and I saluted him.

"Ja, Gott," he mumbled and half-smiled, enigmatically, meaningfully.

Brittany was quiet. Alsace-Lorrain was quiet. The Ardennes was quiet. And would you believe it? Germany was quiet—except, of course, for the occasional sound of a Russian butchering some hapless native. Only Czechoslovakia was noisy, so there we went, our destination Prague, where at that very moment partisans were tearing up the German occupation. But they needed help, for ground had to be cleared and masses of Germans demilitarized.

We traversed the country as dynamically as we had raced toward Koblenz. An occasional straggler, an occasional sniper, once or twice a lumbering panzer too ill-equipped in fuel to maneuver for any kind of fight. Most of them surrendered. Some of them apparently wanted to die, for they stood their ground and did just that. What a stupid thing to do!

Prague was in the distance. Then word came. The partisans had control of most of the sectors of the city. Then another message. World War II was over. But other problems were just about to begin. As we drove around the outskirts of Prague, the whole goddamn German army came up out of nowhere. They were screaming, howling, crying, laughing, and most of all begging, begging to be taken prisoner by the Americans. During that week eighty thousand Germans attempted to give themselves up, and we had to take them, all of them.

The little towns outside Prague looked like an international bazaar—or, more accurately, an Oktoberfest to which George Patton and a few Czechs had been invited. It was an interminable melee. Germans of all ranks were milling about the streets, waylaying Americans and gesticulating to each other. Little by little, we took them in, set up headquarters, and waited for an instructive order. Finally the Communists, who had facilities set up for prisoner induction, approached from the east. Just turn them over to the Russians. Nice and easy, right? Wrong, very wrong!

As soon as word got around that the Russians were coming, the world, which had been rushing headlong at us like an avalanche, turned itself right around and strove to defy all laws of gravity by hurling itself outward, away from us. Some of the prisoners panicked; innumerable others made a more lucid attempt to escape. And we had to stop them. At least twenty were shot and killed during this period; as for the rest of the eighty thousand, either they were apprehended as they made for the gates, or they simply forced us to bust our horns guarding them. Finally, the Russians arrived and relieved us. There had been one German who had delivered a long and somewhat famous farewell the day before.

He was a middle-aged colonel, a career man but also a member of the Nazi party. He had arranged a privilege with an American counterpart to visit the outside for a few hours; he promised he would not escape and left behind all his valuables as collateral. For some reason his word was accepted—

and he was not, in fact, lying. He didn't try to escape. He called for his mistress and shot her, then he murdered an aide who had been released with him. Then he did a very simple thing. He put the barrel of his gun into his mouth and pulled the trigger.

What haunts me most about this event is the way in which it foreshadows the suicide of Adolph Hitler, who took Goebbels and Eva Braun with him. Indeed, a kind of montage formulates itself in my mind. I see artillery blasting all hell out of the sky and infantry pouring across a field in a limitless stream. At the top of the montage is the harsh face of George Patton, barking orders. Superimposed on the picture, just beneath Patton's gaze, is the infamous bunker, and as Patton yells louder and louder, Hitler blows his brains out.

Hitler was dead. Roosevelt was dead. John Wood was gone. Patton was relieved. The war had outlasted all of them. We drove back to Germany to reinforce the incipient occupation. Here, the Russians were more of a problem than they had been in Czechoslovakia. At one point I pulled guard duty in front of a detention camp in which we were holding some five hundred women. Three or four drunken, abusive Russians approached me, and demanded to be let in. There was no lust in their eyes; only meanness. One of them lurched toward me and I whipped my rifle into his face. He drew back. "One more foot forward," I said slowly, gesturing to ensure his comprehension, "and I'll kill you." Baby, I meant it!

And then I was released from duty with the 4th Armored Division. Never again would I see the inside of a tank. I was alive! My God, I was alive! The thought didn't strike me all at once like a thunderbolt. No, it crept up on me slowly, like a gradual chill. But it was nonetheless as stupefying as if suddenly an enormous hand had written YOU'RE ALIVE YOU'RE ALIVE NAT FRANKEL YOU'RE ALIVE across the impalpable surface of the sky.

So I was not about to let myself get killed now. I could have, though. I was assigned to Detach Service with the CIA (at the time an outgrowth of the old OSS). Our task was to hunt up Nazi war criminals: SS men, concentration camp heavies, political hardnoses, etc. And these guys could get dangerous. All desperate men are dangerous. How much more so when in less threatening circumstances they had earned their daily bread busting heads? So we took it easy. We took no chances. We did our job only when circumstances threw it into our faces. I had paid all my dues. After surviving a year of Armageddon, why should I get myself killed by some maniac who's trying to get his ass to Argentina? Fuck it, Argentina deserves him! In retrospect, I'm glad that we—I say we, for no one I knew in Detach Service was ever stupid enough to take any chances— relaxed as much as we did. My God, what if I had really done a good job? I might have deprived NASA of some of its best technicians, or, even worse, United States Steel might have lost some very reliable customers.

No, I had been inside a burning building for an entire year. Walls and floors had been reduced to cinder around me, and the exit to the fresh air, the smokeless expanses of peace, had always been too far ahead even to dream about. Yet there was one occasion upon which circumstance did thrust "duty" before me. An SS lieutenant had been spotted in a small hotel along the Danube. Five of us surrounded the building and ordered him to surrender. My stomach was jumping. Shit, I didn't want to die then! And, of all the goddamn things, he tried to sneak out past—guess who?—me! "Hold it," I cried, and when he whirled around too quickly, I fired. He wasn't up for a shoot-out, however, which was lucky because I had only winged his shoulder. He, on the other hand, had a clear five seconds in which to blast my guts away. But instead he used that interval to drop his pistol and fling up his arms.

"Come and get it," I called to my four comrades.

Oh, fun and games with the CIA! We made our raids mainly in the small towns where the war criminals were scrupulously avoiding the occupational zones and omnipresent Allied troops of the larger cities. At this time, the CIA impressed me as an organization of conscientious altruism with a dedicated sense of mission not merely to extend American influence but to countervail against any force that could be construed as totalitarian. I had little to do with these early pioneers of the CIA—the men who had been with it when I was still at Pine Camp—but I liked them and I trusted them. It was thus no surprise to me to learn that the great antiwar activist, Reverend Coffin of Yale, had been connected with the CIA as late as 1950.

I was, despite my favorable impressions, wholly unwilling to die for the CIA. Yet it was fun in some ways and certainly of more than passing interest. I learned, for example, how to spot an SS man. Lift up his arm and you'll see a little tattoo, something between a mark and a design, in his armpit. Of course, the Germans have always been fond of initiating men into clubs and cults with these kinds of brands. It's very pagan, not altogether unlike the ordeals American college boys must endure to earn fraternity membership.

In many cases, these SS men had lots of money hidden away. I'll tell you a heartbreaker. Two Nazis had been captured trying to buy food. We were ordered to locate their hideout and clean it up. We found it. Myself, a Lieutenant Levy from the 4th Armored, and a captain—let's call him Thompson. Their room was on the upper floor of an inn. It was unoccupied. But Levy noticed an indentation in the wall. He pushed on it, and the whole thing slid. The Nazis had obviously spent hours constructing this little device.

Hmmm, interesting. Levy stuck his hand inside and pulled out a cloth-covered chest that contained about a million dollars worth of jewels. Not a half million. Not two million. A million. Levy and I felt like pirates, khaki Captain Kidds running our lustful hands through a small puddle of rubies, diamonds, platinum, emeralds, onyx, you name it. But Thompson, goddamn him, remained aloof, serious. A man with a future in the military. A by-the-book man. A schmuck, in other words!

We didn't waste any time. Haven't we earned it? we pleaded. Who's going to know? We'll all be rich, we'll go home with something besides veteran benefits and a futile dream of a medallion cab.

"This belongs with the authorities," said Thompson sternly.

"Christ," said Levy, "they'll only steal it themselves." Which was perfectly true.

"What the hell," I said, "you think they're going to use it to feed starving orphans?"

"Forget it, fellas," said Thompson, and he meant it.

The worst part of it all was the timing. Had there been a war outside, had it been possible for Thompson to have taken a slug from a German rifle, I would have shot him dead on the spot. No German had ever hurt me more.

Do I mean it? Would I really have shot an American officer in order to divide up a million dollars with Levy, in order for two dogface Jews to take unto themselves a fortune that had probably been stolen from Jews in the first place? Would I have *really* shot him? Well, I swear on my mother's grave I would have, and right through the neck!

But Levy and I had some drinks instead—drinks and points. Points were earned by soldiers in accordance with combat time, medals, marital status, children, wounds, and so on. And enough points earned you a free boat ride to the United States. Cammerrary and Saville had gone home before me; Paul Glaz had flown back. Now it was my turn. All sufficiently pointed 4th Armored men still in Europe joined the ranks of the 9th Armored, a seasoned, fiery outfit with whom I was proud to return. We landed at Newport News; it wasn't Ellis Island, but it worked in a pinch.

One year later I went to the first reunion of the 4th Armored Division. I've been to thirty since. The next one will be in

Orlando—Orlando, Florida, where once again the last of the best will congregate, a handful of sere warriors who can now only contemplate the Cold War and détente, organization man and intellectual rebellion, An Loc and the march on Washington, Watergate and porno and race riots, with sad and mute bewilderment.

# Appendix A: Officers

Why would I, in a book devoted to a ground-level view of the 4th Armored Division, bother to spend more than a couple of pages describing the military command posts that oversaw us? The reason is this: In remembering and judging the men who had tactical control of my life, I am using a particular criterion. It is a criterion eminently suitable to any view of war from up front.

What makes the good ones good and the bad ones bad? What is the difference between an officer for whom we would die and another whom we would just as soon kill? It is, in the long run, the extent to which they share the common lot of their men. Are they distant, protected, scrubbed clean, sterile? If so, they are nothing but computers issuing indifferent orders. Or are they accessible, exposed to the gamut of danger and misfortune, with dirt in their fingernails and an instinctive understanding of and respect for our view of the world? If so, they become one with their units. The leader and the led fuse into one body. The legs answer the needs of the pelvis, which works when the brain tells it to—and the brain registers pain when an arm is mutilated.

In one sense, a good officer is nothing more than an extension of his men. He is *of* them; that post of high power is being occupied by a dog soldier himself, whom circumstance and necessity have flung from the trench to the corridors of decision. Of course, in another sense, the officer has to be a very different sort of fellow, with intellectual and personal skills marking a distinctly commanding caste. He has to be both; he must be dog soldier *and* Brahmin. The order is a tall one indeed—which no doubt accounts for the extreme paucity of good officers in this or any army.

Many men go through a war without ever knowing or seeing a good leader. My impression of World War I is that you can count with one hand the number of decent officers on either side. World War II was better, and we in the 4th Armored were lucky; we saw upwards of five officers who ranged in type from competent to great. And I imagine that the Pacific theater abounded with notable commanders. Perhaps the increased sophistication of modern warfare from one world war to the next served as a fillip to the emergence of far greater numbers of far better soldiers.

We had three division commanders. The first was John Wood, the father of the 4th Armored Division. Wood was *the* exception to the typically derogatory remarks GIs naturally tend to make about officers in general. From June 18, 1942, to December 3, 1944, when he was relieved of his command, I would not hear one even slightly critical remark from any man who served under him. The extent to which any officer excels is directly proportional to the extent of his similarity to John Shirley Wood. Patton was a great general, but Patton was something of a freak. Wood was just great.

Indeed, the story of his ouster has never been, and probably never will be, accurately documented. Wood did not make an issue of it, but it is commonly known that he privately derided the "ill health" bullshit handed down by Ike and Patton. After he was fired, a more believable explanation was leaked from headquarters; the newspapers, however, never picked up on it for fear of compromising either Patton, Ike, or Wood's successors. Yet most of the soldiers in the 4th Armored heard it, and most of them, myself included, believed it—and still do.

We had just captured Arracourt when the orders came down to penetrate into Alsace-Lorraine and close the Belfort Gap. Patton ordered Wood to spearhead the attack.

"Dammit, George, we're not robots. We need a rest!"

"John, you're getting soft!"

And that was it. It may be that Patton saw Wood as a threat to his personal domination of the Third Army and was just looking for an excuse to get rid of him. Or maybe—who knows, Patton could get strange at times—he actually thought that Wood *was* getting soft and that the 4th Armored deserved to be commanded by a man who would drive it more ruthlessly and thereby exploit its full potentialities. In any case, it was a bad, bad deal, a testament to either vainglory or unadulterated misjudgment. But George Patton, in whom destructive vanity mingled so deeply with genuine greatness, was the subject of an earlier chapter.

The fact that Patton saw Wood more as a personal threat is borne out not merely by Wood's unique ability to confront Patton where necessary but also by the sycophantic role played by General Gaffey, Wood's successor. There was nothing wrong with Gaffey; in most particulars he was a good soldier. But from December 3 to March 23 of the next year, when Gaffey, no longer useful to Patton, was relieved, there was very little buffer between us and the top dog. Patton ran our division during those days as he never could when Wood was in the driver's seat. And after Gaffey came a competent division commander named William Hoge, who led us to the end of the war. But even Hoge was something of a stopgap. When history remembers the 4th Armored Division, it remembers John Wood.

Another reason for Wood's dismissal was no doubt his refusal to play politics with other officers. He certainly des-

pised Thomas Churchill, who took command of the 8th Battalion just about the time Wood was relieved. Churchill,
despite the fact that his name is spread around history texts
as if he were the real vanguard of the Singling push, was
incompetent. But he was also a polished cocktail party game-
player type, college and ROTC bred, who yessed his way to a
command and who probably impressed his superiors with a
suave public relations capacity. Alas, the soldiers of the 8th
Tank Battalion were not part of his public, and neither was
John Wood. At one point, someone probably had to decide
between them, and Churchill won the game. I imagine,
however, that both Ike and Patton wound up regretting it
because Churchill didn't last long. They had to kick him
upstairs somewhere. So what was the result? A few weeks of
impotent battalion command coupled with the irrevocable
loss of a supremely talented divisional leader!

Before Churchill was given the battalion, we had Edgar
Conley, who was eventually promoted. It was Conley who
gave his battalion the apt name of "the rolling eight ball."
Conley was a superb officer, albeit a somewhat gruff and
frequently unreasoning man. Yet he was far too professional
ever to let personality—his, or someone he may have taken a
dislike to—interfere with duty. And duty includes fairness. In
fact, I was one man of whom Conley had a negative opinion.
And to tell you the truth, I wasn't exactly enthused about his
manners, either. This fact ought to indicate, if anything, how
really fine a soldier he was, for I certainly have no particular
need to sing his praises. But truth is truth, and truth is on his
side.

Our antipathy went back almost all the way to the beginning, to Camp Ibis. I had an illegal car on base. When time
came to ship out, I approached Conley and asked him if I
could drive it to safety. "I don't care if that fucking car rots!"
Conley roared back. And rot it did. But this was the same man
who was later able to joke about getting shot in the ass—well,
if not joke, at least not take it as a personal affront to his

exalted stature. Oh, that it could have been Thomas Churchill with lead in his behind! He probably would have written a letter of complaint about it to Franklin Roosevelt.

After Churchill came Albin Irzyk, who was to the 8th Battalion what John Wood was to the 4th Armored. In fact, Irzyk was a perfect example of what I have indicated, that the quality of a leader is in direct proportion to his similarity to Wood. I think about men like Wood and Irzyk, and I realize that the one fact that stands out, aside from their intelligence, compassion, and courage, is that they saved lives, scores of lives.

Unlike Churchill, Irzyk looked like a soldier, not a computer programmer. Like Wood, he was stocky, robust, and alive with contagious energy. Irzyk also remembered the first names of every soldier he ever encountered in his unit. That may seem a bit prosaic; you may even think it somewhat patronizing on the part of the officer. After all, we couldn't call him by *his* first name. But you have to put yourself in the context of a war. This isn't an insurance company we're talking about. You're alone, you're nothing, this thing you've got that you presume to call your life can be blown away at any second. And then you're a number. Maybe they give you the Purple Heart. In fact, they probably will. Big deal! We used to call the Purple Heart the German marksmanship medal.

So every little bit counts. Friendship. Humor. Some sense of adventure. And an officer who knows your name. That counts a lot. I see Irzyk from time to time at army reunions; he lives in Florida now. Now I do call him by his first name. And he still remembers every soldier with whom he had direct contact, including the dead ones. My moral imagination is not deep enough to assess the personal responsibility an officer bears for the human beings who die under his command. But whatever that responsibility is, I'm sure that Irzyk's personalization of his command served it. The refusal to dehumanize bodies— maybe that's the mark of an officer who is also a man. If that is the case, Albin Irzyk was the paragon of the human warrior.

The military, however, is the military, and Irzyk was Catholic. That's not as bad as being Jewish or black, but if your family happens to eat fish on Friday, you can expect a much lower career ceiling. (Unless, of course, you're fighting for the IRA. But we're still talking about Uncle Sam.) Occasionally, the powers that be will condescend, and a black like Ben Davis is allowed to climb the ladder. And perhaps a few Catholics here and there, provided they don't *look* too Catholic. But it's like winning a lottery. The tragic and wasteful fact of the matter remains the same. I am personally convinced that Albin Irzyk ought to be sitting with the Joint Chiefs of Staff at this very moment. At the very least, he, not Gaffey, should have replaced Wood as division commander.

So our division began with a giant and our battalion ended with one. Our company commanders were, of course, more amorphous, particularly since company commanders have a tendency to get shot. I cannot speak of any but my own, which was Company C. Eugene Bush was the first; we called him the greyhound because he was always running somewhere. Well, why not? The whole goddamn Third Army was also always running. After Bush was a fellow named Stevenson, a decent, competent man. He was wounded at Singling and replaced by a great soldier named DeRosa, mentioned earlier in this narrative. Then Stevenson returned and finished the war with us.

There was one other preeminent officer whom I got to know fairly well after the war. He was the commander of the 37th Tank Battalion; his name was Creighton Abrams. Though I never fought with him, we of the 8th always respected him; his reputation as a master tactician was well established before the end of the war. And no one from the 37th that I've met has ever disputed that reputation.

He was a quiet, friendly, unassuming man. And we of the 4th Armored would watch him die. The medical verdict was lung cancer, but cancer has many names. One of those names is Vietnam. We'd see him at reunions once a year. At the beginning, throughout the fifties, he was the picture of health and whatever it is that we mean when we say contentment. Then came Da Nang. Hue. Tonkin. Haiphong. All those horrific names, names that carry the same connotations in New York or Portland that Bastogne carries in Berlin or Iwo Jima in Tokyo. His face grew drawn; he grew more silent—but never taciturn, never unfriendly. Finally, we all knew he was dying. It was like being back on the battlefield cradling a fatally wounded soldier in your arms. No hope, not even with every damn divisional medic in attendance.

And he'd seldom talk about Vietnam. When the subject came up—as it did once in a private conversation I had with him—he would say what they were all probably saying. If only the politicians would untie our hands! Nat, you have no idea of the political crap we're dealing with! I can't even tell you! Christ, if they'd let us alone, we'd force the North to settle in Paris. Don't ask me what's making them stop us. I can't even begin to tell you! Christ, I could win it!

Well, I know what all the "experts" have had to say, but I tend to agree with Abrams, and I bitterly mourn the war that poisoned his lungs. I wasn't in Vietnam; I wasn't personally involved in any of the domestic upheavals that accompanied the war. But in my own way I was very close to it, if only by watching this noble warrior fail and die from one frustrated year to the next. No way could such a man expect such a future, not after rolling a whole battalion across Germany like a gladiator in a chariot.

Indeed, I am personally fascinated, perhaps preoccupied, with the eventual futures of the men with whom I fought. This man is a truck driver; that man is a stockbroker. I think I know the source of my fascination. When you do not expect to have any future at all, the fact that you do finally have one seems gratuitous, like a special gift from God. There's something unreal about it. The fact that Andy Cammerrary is now a baker has a special significance, even though there are a million others like him. Eugene Bush is now running a marina in New Jersey. Irzyk is in quiet retirement. Abrams's future was as dark as it was earth-shattering. And yet they're all sort of intangible, the contractors and the policemen, the bus drivers and the commercial artists, like roles enacted on a stage that's been loosened from its moorings to float in the sky, aimlessly but courageously.

General John S. Wood looked like a bull who huffs and snorts, stamps his feet, lowers his head, charges, wins the match—and then embraces the matador. Somewhere in Brittany two soldiers were standing around and joking. One of them punctuated his story by affecting the voice and mannerisms of a homosexual. Wood happened to be standing behind them. When the soldiers saw him, they snapped to attention, a little concerned about what their pugnacious commander had overheard. "At ease, men," Wood said. "My middle name happens to be Shirley." And then he walked away, looking, as always, like a tank in motion. Christ, John Wood could not have been the commander of any other kind of division but an armored one.

The key to understanding and appreciating John Wood is the word *balance*. I have said that he was capable of being both dog soldier and master planner; he saw things from both the basement and from Olympus. It is not easy to keep those two worlds in focus, to function in both, to relate to the needs of both. If the scale is tipped in either direction, someone will suffer somewhere. The leader becomes aloof; the mystical fusion between leader and led is broken, and the great masses of the led are no longer impelled to perform the necessary deeds in the necessary places. Or the leader becomes so much a mere extension of his men that the great vulcanizing force that is able to see all the forests for all the trees is sterilized. But in John Wood we had a man who could almost magically maintain the vital equilibrium. The Greeks would have admired Wood more than Patton, for balance was a key to all the values that that civilization propounded. Wood was the perfect Greek hero, like something etched on an old frieze. On the other hand, for all his genius, a genius labyrinthine in substance, George Patton was *unbalanced.* In fact, he was crazy. By contrast, Wood was magnificently lucid. His were the clear eyes that foresee and make possible the sober erection of civilizations.

But Wood balanced himself across a yet more precipitous gulf. The role of division commander may be the hardest one to fill, harder even than army commander. The latter is often a pure strategist. He moves lines and flags around on a map. He chooses the men to head the actual units, but that's as far as his tactical acumen need extend. He may, in fact, be a great tactician, but he doesn't have to be. The division commander *must* be both. His role begins in that murky area between strategy and tactics. He has to know why he is doing what he is doing, or else the coordination between his division and the larger picture is endangered; he must also counsel the army commanders, tell them how the tactical picture affects the strategic one. If he doesn't, a Patton or a Rommel may write what is on paper a beautiful concerto, but no one, even a Horowitz with a thousand fingers, will ever be able to play it.

And if the division commander cannot actually win the battles counted on by the strategist, forget it! So not only must his strategic feedback be profound, he must be wholly responsible for tactical factors as well. He, not the battalion commanders, must have the real knowledge of the enemy, the real command of supply and administrative factors, of topographical exigencies, and of coordination within the division. It may be an impossible job; it may be to army commander what a mayor's job is to the President's. Can it be done? Well, New York had LaGuardia, and the 4th Armored had Wood.

Again, excellence through balance! Wood was the greatest tactician of the European theater and a brilliant strategic thinker as well. Both Wood and Patton have been criticized for not bothering to take Lorient in Brittany. Had we taken it and other towns like it, so the argument goes, we would never have had the supply problems that plagued us later on. It is a respectable argument, particularly since supply problems would indeed be our worst hindrance by the time late 1944 rolled around. It is a respectable argument, but an erroneous one.

First of all, we never could have taken these towns in time to speed up the war. Thousands would have died rather need-lessly. The time we actually wasted waiting for supplies was nothing compared to the time we would have spent—not to mention the energy we would have used, and probably lost forever—taking even three towns like Lorient. No, I remember Metz too well. It is true that that city was extraordinarily well-fortified, but the three months Patton spent in taking it were still exorbitant. Cut that time in half for the other towns, and we're still farting away a month and a half each time! And then you've got to worry about keeping lines between the town and the troops open to permit the transportation of supplies! Never mind!

The fact is, it was Wood, the tactician, who first saw this most crucial strategic problem. We were outside Lorient ready to lay siege when Wood contacted Patton and protested. And Patton agreed. The job of isolating Lorient was turned over to a more dispensable unit, and we directed our ultimate sights toward Germany. The original scheme, which was to regroup gradually on the Seine, was dropped. At Wood's behest Patton sent us screaming and speeding and roaring on our way.

It is equally important to point out that Wood was not merely a master tactician but an innovative one as well. The importance of the 4th derives a great deal from the way in which we epitomized the classic armored unit—in much the same way that Caesar's Tenth Legion epitomized the warfare of classic antiquity. It was Wood who made the oral command common currency, who encouraged the quick order, and cultivated all officers he felt were capable of making such speedy decisions. He added to this a fetish for constant aerial cover (not many of us would be killed by bombs or bullets flung from the sky) and a fanatical insistence on continuous movement. These developments define the armored division. As such, he wasn't merely the father of the 4th but the father of the very concept we embodied.

And embody it we would, with formations devised by this former athlete, who could well have been born on the playing fields of Eton. Wood always had the engineers up front, two truckloads of equipment behind, artillery forward but behind the lead, and, in the middle of it all, tanks rolling in pairs as if in parody of some strange technological wedding ceremony. In fact, we used to say the tanks were "married up." And no tank would be allowed to stop unless ordered to do so. If the lead tank stalls, you drive around it, into a ditch if necessary, and then "coil," as it was called, into a reassembly area. But never stop. He taught us that to stop was to die. And if you're waiting for gasoline, don't breathe until you get it!

Strategist and tactician, dog soldier and superman: balanced, always balanced. If Patton's name conjures up Alexander's or Caesar's or some other mythic figure, Wood was Lee and Stonewall Jackson, Francis Marion and Wellington and Francis Drake. We called him Tiger Jack. Why? Because he roared at the Germans? Because he pounced on the enemy and dragged them off to a goddamn lair someplace? No, not quite. We called him Tiger Jack because it was common knowledge that when Patton roared at John Wood, John Wood paced back and forth and gave it right back to him. And what paces and roars if not a tiger? No, John Wood was never a legend. He was something greater than that; he was a human being capable of confronting a legend and holding his own.

And "P" Wood, we called him that, too. Actually, that one went back to West Point, where he often tutored less gifted classmates. "P" was West Point jargon for "professor." Notice how both his nicknames reflect his essential humanness. He gave hell to the Germans, but none of that found its way into either moniker. Now, I don't want this to sound like some kind of a damn testimonial or some slavish crock of hero worship. When he sat on a toilet, John Wood didn't shit vanilla ice cream any more than I do. But I have to emphasize his greatness, I have to sketch it as well as I can. Perhaps it is more important for me to do so than it is to expand even upon the greatness of the division itself. After all, there were bastards in the 4th Armored Division. There are bastards everywhere. But our commander was not adulterated like that, at least not as far as we were concerned. I don't know how he treated his wife or his fourth cousin, and I don't care. The qualities he brought to Europe with him were exemplary.

It was natural, never forced or contrived, for him to live with and like the men. After all, the leader and the led had fused—and that's no mere figure of speech! He sloshed in the mud, slept outside, and took the same rude baths we took. Captured food and liquor seldom got to the officers; we got it. And how he hated to see us die! Glory is fine, but more so for the ones who live to enjoy it. That's where men like Wood are very, very different from the Pattons, or even the U.S. Grants. Grant never strove to spare hardship; consider his slow move through Virginia. But for Wood preventing useless suffering was a paramount aspect of leadership itself. The glory, moreover, belonged with the division: no ivory-handled guns for him! So if you've never heard of John Wood, it was probably because he was a better soldier than most of the ones you have heard of.

Like Edgar Conley, Wood did not start off his command with any effort to win friends and influence soldiers. At Ibis he ordered us to march with our sleeves down and our collars buttoned. And that was the Mojave, baby! But discipline like that is easier to swallow when it's imposed by a man who treats you with extraordinary respect in every other vital particular. He doted on initiative. Privates ought to act like corporals where appropriate—and corporals like lieutenants, and so forth on up to the top. End result: The 4th Armored produced as many future generals as any fighting unit in American history.

And Wood's future? He got himself a replacement center command for armored units in Fort Knox. It must have been a bad backslide for him, not only training raw recruits but doing so in a place where the 4th Armored had nearly two years earlier whipped itself into shape. He retired in 1946. Now, when Bradley retired, he sold Bulova watches. Wood joined a governmental organization for refugees and ran the Germany-Austria branch. He stayed in Austria until 1951.

Then, more of the same. He joined another refugee reconstruction agency after the European theater was fully closed; this time it was in Korea, where there had been, I recall, another war of sorts. Then a civil defense job in Reno, where he had settled to live. His body could no longer sustain his inherent restlessness, so his mind took up the slack. Without ever being "political" in the sense of a MacArthur, Wood developed a comprehension of world affairs comparable to a Marshall's or a Zumwalt's. He died in 1966.

Wood's postwar career befits the man. He was a humanist. He did not dote on war for its own sake, as did Patton. It is something ugly, and Wood knew this as well as Gandhi did. But somehow humanity comes to a fork in the road when war is necessary. Once that necessity is recognized, certain values —American values of personal freedom—must be preserved throughout; and certain individual characteristics, a certain mixture of valor and compassion, must be maintained. When the war is over, you don't stop fighting. You house refugees. You develop an awareness of present threats, and you devise the best ways to handle them. Whatever you do is part of a larger picture. War and peace have that in common.

Now I'll tell you a story. There were two hard-boiled bastards in Company B. They had gotten friendly with each other back at Ibis, and by the time we were fighting for some damn nameless village not far from Arracourt, they had become blood brothers. One day a shell unexpectedly blasted in our direction; a piece of it took out one of the two friends. Right out. Dead. His buddy—I think his name was Kenny Morgan—cursed like a pimp. He kicked the tank, snarled at everyone around him. Shit, shit, he hissed. But he didn't cry.

Some time later I heard that John Wood had been relieved. Nobody really knew why, not yet. But the smell of petty politics, of personal jealousy and backstabbing, was in the air. I happened to be walking toward the spot where Company B was sacking out for a few hours for a little sleep, a little uncharacteristic immobility. I saw the man who had hissed shit above his broken brother-in-arms; he was leaning against his tank, smoking a cigarette.

And the little bastard was crying.

# Appendix B:
# Soldiers

George Spires.

He was the best mess sergeant in the history of the 4th Armored. He dominated our stomachs from Normandy to Singling as powerfully as John Wood dominated our lives or Roosevelt our destinies. Nothing *too* fancy. You don't have time for beef stroganoff in the middle of a war. But of course there were those fine occasions when luxury items captured from the SS were available, and George exploited those occasions to the fullest. It was our tendency to drink every bottle of wine we could get our hands on; George would then become our adversary, hopping from tank to tank and sometimes throwing a punch or two in order to grab off a fine vintage and hurry it back to the kitchen. Because George liked to cook with wine. You'd have to fight him for sherry, and cognac could lead to blood. Once he marinated a vat of chicken livers with brandy. Very, very good.

"Shit," a redneck complained while eating a piece, "you can't get drunk from these things."

"Slob," George hissed.

And if he liked you, oh boy! "How do you like your hamburgers?" he asked me once.

"Medium rare," I said jokingly, as if I cared about the preparation of any other cut of meat besides porterhouse. But the hamburger turned out better than many porterhouses. Brown-red meat sizzling in its own juices! And don't ask the man for ketchup because he's liable to shoot you.

Did I say Normandy to Singling? Alas, I did. If you recall, the Battle of Singling was marked by the presence of many noncombatants stuck hopelessly in combatant's shoes. George Spires was asked to command a tank—imagine, *command* one!—and he accepted. There was no one else around at the time, and we needed every machine available. Well, George couldn't shoot his way out of a frozen condom, but his gallantry was as refined as his palate. His tank swerved badly from side to side, and then his treading was blown out. He jumped out of the turret and landed on his back. He got up again to race for cover, but a crackle of German fire ended his flight.

George would live another twenty years and even raise a daughter. But his entire left side was paralyzed. Most of his life after the war was an affair of veterans' hospitals, a numbingly long tenure in one, release to temporary freedom, and then another hospital, and another, and another. I lost touch with George Cardge's widow, for she lives in Wheeling, West Virginia, but Mrs. Spires is in my neck of the woods, and I visit her frequently. She runs a little store, and is managing to live out her own life in quiet dignity. I think of her like a sister. The daughter is happily married, a source of joy. I barely know her, but I guess she'd be my niece.

I even liked his name, Spires. You build your best cathedrals in your own gut, and the men who remember you savor that memory more fundamentally than the vision of the brightest stained glass.

Constant Klinga.

The man who said, "So they got us surrounded again, the poor bastards!" thereby hanging an instantaneously resonant dog tag on his whole division.

"Hey Nat, did I ever tell you about the time I got laid on a pool table?"

"I don't want to hear about it."

"It was just me and the bartender in a little joint on Flatbush Avenue. I'm messin' around the pool table, sipping a beer. In walks this redhead with enormous tits and her hair piled on her head like a haystack."

"Forget it, Klinga!"

"I see her out of the corner of my eye. 'Eight ball in the side pocket,' I says. 'You're pretty good, aren't you?' she says. 'It ain't so hard when you got a big stick,' I says. Do you get it, Nat? I'm talkin' about the pool stick, but—hell, big stick!—I was also talkin' about my cock!"

"I get it, Klinga! I get it!"

"I ask the bartender if he minds. He don't mind. I'm a regular. So she climbs up on the pool table, those big titties waving out over the side, and, Nat, my friend, she spread 'em, she spread 'em wide!"

"Klinga, would you shut up?"

During the heavy fighting around Jena, just after the liberation of Ohrdruf, Constant Klinga was manning the gun in his turret. A single German bullet struck him in the forehead, and he died at once. That's the way a man like Constant Klinga ought to die—so quickly he has no consciousness of death itself. All life, all life, until the very last second of life.

Tom Riordan.

Tom was an infantryman from Chicago assigned to the 4th Armored. He was very Irish Catholic and an inordinately, almost exorbitantly, thoughtful man. Religion for him was never a matter of ritual. It was a long and painful process whereby a man examines his relationship with the world and tries to make some sense of it. Such a man doesn't belong in war. He belongs in a seminary; in fact, Tom had studied in one, but changed his mind in 1941, the first year of the only war he ever could have agreed to fight in.

I knew him as a private, though he eventually went home a corporal. I remember once just after Bastogne he was sitting not far from me. At the time my face was sweaty and probably mud spattered.

"I hope all this is worth it," he said.

"Of course, it's worth it," I said.

"Only time will tell," he said.

I haven't seen Riordan since the war; not actually a member of the 4th Armored, he doesn't come to our reunions. But I'd like to see him and find out what he's been doing. And I'd like to hear his opinion. About whether or not it was worth it.

Sometimes I think we lost more men celebrating the end of the war than we did in combat. The rooftops were big spots for drinking, and copulating, and carousing—and neither roof nor man was any too sturdy. Many were the souls who fell. Amen.

And there were fights galore. A different kind of fighting, to be sure. The combat of the last year, or, for that matter, any combat, is tension building, not tension releasing. Controlled mayhem can be deadly. You have to have your catharses on cue. You're nervous, nervous, nervous, and then you fight an anonymous enemy—which builds up more tension even as it releases some—and the fight ends slowly, so slowly you have to be on your guard as the enemy withdraws. More tension. Then the whole goddamn thing ends, and you're a wreck. So what do you do to save yourself?

You fight!

I remember one brawl that occurred as we were pulling back into Germany from Czechoslovakia. Two privates were whaling like hell. One of the men went down. The other stood above him, grinning like a devil. He started stomping on the man's face. By the time I reached him and pulled him away, his adversary's face was oatmeal. Another few minutes and he'd have been dead.

War kills its legions, and so does the end of a war. I'll tell you about a couple.

Pop Cronan was probably drinking more in 1945 than he had been in 1944. When the war ended, he disappeared into a bottle. I found him once under a jeep, awash in a puddle of his own vomit. Others found him at various times in similar situations. On a roof, shouting obscenities at the sky. In a whorehouse, terrorizing the employees with broken glass. In a tavern, being funny for the locals. They probably couldn't understand a word of what he was saying, but his cavorting was inevitably Chaplinesque, and gesture is a universal language.

Pop Cronan came home in late 1945. He had nothing to do. He got a few jobs in gas stations in Virginia, but he drank and the customers complained. So Pop was fired. Soon he stopped trying. The denouement consisted of two chapters—the rural and the urban. Most of us live one or the other, and our lives are thus one half the history of the nation itself. But some of us, like Pop Cronan, drift despairingly from country to city, trying to survive, trying to see where the best chances are. Chances for what? Tranquillity? Booze? Work? Love? Or freedom? But what the hell is freedom? From farm to smokestack Pop Cronan lived the life of his nation.

The towns depressed Cronan, but he needed them. You can't ask passing trees for spare change. So Birmingham. So Montgomery. So Atlanta. Soon there would be no more gin; there was never enough time or cash for gin. Wine, cheap wine, and the company of men who had not fought in Europe because the army wouldn't have taken them. In fact, most of them didn't even know there had been a war. Jackson. Baton Rouge. Biloxi. But stay away from New Orleans. You get killed in New Orleans.

Cronan slugged at some wine, and started hiking down a highway that led beyond Lake Charles, toward the dense Louisiana wilderness. The wilderness wasn't bad when you were stocked up—and Pop was stocked up, with three shorties of muscatel in his back and hip pockets. Soon he was alone. No cars. In the near distance a railroad track, and Pop, who knew the country better than the city, figured there'd be shelter around. A hobo joint. Or an abandoned shack. There was a shack, as it turned out, its corroded wood hanging like splintered vines toward the center, threatening complete if lazy collapse.

Cronan climbed into the shack and drank down one bottle. The other two he left at his feet. He stared hard at them. That's one of the greatest pleasures for a man like Cronan: being drunk and not only knowing that he's got more but contemplating and savoring the vision of that supply. It stabilizes the future for him. But then it started to rain.

The Louisiana rain is a cold son of a bitch in December; it goes right through you, wine or no wine. Pop didn't know what to do. The shack wasn't much help; the rain was coming through, and the cold was settling everywhere—everywhere he was was cold, like it was following him. Might as well walk. He drank the other two bottles fast, too fast. He wandered out, but the wine was dizzying, and he probably had a cold as well. Black, black. He fell into the warmth of oblivion, but his bed was the cold steel of the railroad track. The Midnight Special roared by and cut him to his death.

The bitterness in George Patton's mouth was heavy after his command was abrogated. But not too heavy. After all, he had had his triumph, and the world knew it. He had glory to bask in. Hammelburg was hush-hush, and there was no one in the Allied camp—not Ike, not the despised Montgomery, and certainly not Bradley—whose name could command such instant awe. But Patton had another problem. He had nothing to do.

Well, they gave Patton something to do. They put him in charge of the Fifteenth Army, whose task it was to write the history of World War II. Is that called "kicked upstairs"? Kicked indeed! Patton himself didn't bother with the research or the typing. He traveled around, visiting small towns that he had liberated, which were more than anxious to celebrate his presence with dinner parties, street fairs, and the like. Maybe he almost enjoyed it. And he did a lot of hunting, which he loved.

A sad George Patton went out one day to pursue his favorite pastime. Patton's aide, General Gay, accompanied him as usual out to the country to net a few birds—a pleasant way to engage the sunset of one's life.

The driver's name was Woodring. There were some busted-out machines lying about. He pointed them out to Gay, shook his head, and said something about the horrors of war—those very horrors somehow redeemed by his own extraordinary stature. Woodring looked briefly at the machines pointed out by his passenger—but not briefly enough.

Not briefly enough. He collided with an oncoming truck. The jeep halted. Gay and Woodring were fine. Patton asked them, you see; Patton asked them first. But Patton was paralyzed, and said so—said so cooly, analytically, with a gallantry at least the equal of any single moment of combat in his life. At that moment he knew he was dead; he knew he'd never settle for a wheelchair and spoon-feeding. He wanted life on his own terms, not merely survival. It was December 9, 1945. Two weeks later he was dead. Patton is crazy—he'll never make Bastogne by Christmas.

Top and bottom, my friend. Soldiers, defined and vitalized and given life by the unending death of war. Pop Cronan wasn't merely a dog soldier with no conception of, let alone effect on, the larger scales up and down which he moved; no, he was even *less* than that. He was a drunken mechanic, a complete nobody who supplies the grease that oils other men's actions. A war machine is a vast, an all-encompassing thing— and Pop's place was at the very bottom, along with the latrine cleaners and stretcher bearers.

George Patton wasn't merely the head of an army. He was,

first of all, the head of *the* army—in fact, of all armies. He was a man who thought he was Alexander the Great and Caesar and William the Conqueror, and whose power and actions made it difficult for anyone to dispute those grandiose self-definitions. In the annals of war, which stretch all the way back to the very beginnings of civilization, George Patton was at the very top.

But you can no more take glory with you than you can muscatel. Finally, glory belongs with the army and the division and the battalion. What the hell is the difference between two corpses? Not much! Oh, they both have their pasts, which storm with nobility and ignominy. The moment of dying is, however, the great equalizer; men are inexorably defined by the manner of their deaths. Two soldiers named Cronan and Patton died the same way, perhaps on the same day, and so merged into one soldier, one tragic man cheated of Valhalla and given instead the bitter Eucharist of decline and anti-climax. There is a strange continuity to all human affairs, of which war and peace are the largest.

# Index